THE CANONGATE PRIZE
FOR NEW WRITING

Writing Wrongs

THE CANONGATE PRIZE
FOR NEW WRITING

Writing Wrongs

Canongate Books
IN ASSOCIATION WITH

First published in Great Britain in 2002 by
Canongate Books Ltd, 14 High Street,
Edinburgh EH1 1TE

10 9 8 7 6 5 4 3 2 1

The publishers acknowledge subsidy from the
Scottish Arts Council towards the publication
of this volume

**For further information about the Canongate Prize for
New Writing, and details of how to enter next year's
competition, please visit:
www.canongateprize.com**

British Library Cataloguing-in-Publication Data
A catalogue record for this book is available
on request from the British Library

ISBN 1 84195 292 3

Book design by James Hutcheson

Typeset by Palimpsest Book Production Ltd,
Polmont, Stirlingshire
Printed and bound by Bookmarque Ltd, Croydon, Surrey

www.canongate.net

Contents

SUZANNE AHERN
Sofía's Story

The call to wake comes early at 6.00 a.m., but my eyes are already open. Sleep did not come easily last night. I am waiting. Enriqueta, my mother, taps softly at the door and then, as I do not answer, she raps a little louder and slowly pushes her head into my room. I see her face illuminated from the side by the ray of brilliant late summer sunshine falling in behind her and my eyes flood with angry tears. Invisible pain. She can't see it as I push my own face deeper into the blanket and murmur, unconvincingly, that I have only just awoken. She leaves the room without speaking a word and I pull myself from the bed to dress. It will be my birthday this time next month.

Outside in the parlour my older brother waits impatiently, kicking his feet absent-mindedly at one leg of our heavy table as she fusses with his collar. 'You must look smart, Jordi,' she mutters at his childishly mute ears, 'we have done nothing to be ashamed of, nothing.'

Today is the day that I am to be returned to my 'real' family.

The February light is bright as I step from the house to join them. Perhaps it is because I was born at this time of year that I believe it to be the most beautiful, and I stop for a second or two to take one last look at our garden and to flick my eyes over our happy family house. The same old question races frantically through my mind, 'Why me? Why me?' but I am never any closer to finding an answer. Today the terror and disgust is so much stronger. I feel the bile rise and fall in bitter waves.

My mother looks at me from far away, long before I have reached the spot where they wait beside the motor car. The motor car with its engine running. Ready. Her eyes are staring hard at me and although I want to look away, I cannot. I love this woman with all my heart. She is my mother.

As I reach her shaking body, heavily wrapped despite the warmth of this radiant Argentine morning, she drops my brother's hand and flings herself around me in a tangle of arms, shawl and unfaltering love. I cry out loud as if shot by a bullet and the pain of separation pierces through me. I have anticipated the arrival of this stabbing ache many times before today but now it is finally here and I slump heavily into her embrace, almost unable to stand. Almost unable to endure this moment. It is a bleak, hard prospect for one so young that I will now suffer this torment every single day of my life ahead. Every single day of my new life with my 'real' family. I hate them already. I do not want to go.

Mother mops my eyes, and I hers, and we climb together into the back of the suffocatingly warm car, snuggled close like desolate lovers. My brother slips silently into the front seat beside my uncle Carlos and none of us speaks on the short journey into the centre of Buenos Aires.

All along the streets near our house, people come out into the road to watch us pass by yet none wave me on. It still confuses me that they react with such a puzzling mixture of fear and intrigue towards me. For years, they spoke not a word to me yet they must have been aware of my adoptive state long before I was. Very few came near me and those that did invariably withdrew their companionship after only a short time. I don't understand why. Do I frighten them? Am I such an unlikeable child? I think I must be.

Mother looks at me with her tear-stained face and, recognising my concern, she whispers, 'They are only jealous, my child, of the life we share and,' she adds, brushing a stray hair from my eyes, 'jealous of the great love your magnificent father had for you when he was still with us. You were our precious gift from God. And they know that,' she says, nodding her head with disdain towards the sombre, sunken faces of the onlookers.

I draw my gaze back to my mother whose hands are still tangled through mine and whose face streams once again with glistening tears, and I bury my head in her shawl. I wish with all my heart that my father was still alive. I wish he was here now, with us in this very car, in his impeccable police uniform. He would frighten off all these ghoulish voyeurs and he would not let this horrendous thing happen to me, his 'precious gift'. He would fight for me, in a way my mother has not been able to. I know he would. There would have been no blood test, no court case and I would not be going back to 'them'. My father would have saved me from them.

But he is dead.

It is not far from our street to the court house. My voice is not my own. It is small and squeaky and I cannot breathe for the scrum of people, the reporters and cameras, and the enormous heaviness pressing down upon my chest.

I sit frozen with fear beside my mother. A little to my left stands the grumbling woman hired by mother who, last time I was here, whisked me into a cold side room for a 'confidential chat'. She told me, wringing her hands in either glee or pain (I was not sure which), that my 'real' mother, Estelle, may very well have been a terrorist. It could not be proven nor discounted, she said.

Today she barely catches my eye but I know she is right. I know today that my cherished mother and father adopted me to save me from the horrors of the subversives and despite the woman finally wishing me well in my new life, I am filled with dread and fear. How can it be right to send me back? How?

'I don't want to go, I don't, I don't, Mama, Mama . . . please,' I cry as they lead me from the court room, but no one seems to be listening. The guards pull on one side of Enriqueta as my 'grandparents' tug at my arm and drag me away from her. This is it, my life is over. The terrorists are taking me away.

It is not far from the court house to my new home.

They treat me like a package. Something gathered up in haste from a lost luggage office. I am touched with extreme caution in case I should break or, worse still, become misplaced again. Their eyes are constantly upon me. The old woman keeps saying gently 'I know, I know,' as I continually squeal that I want my Mama, yet still she takes me away. I can see in her eyes that she will never let me go again. Her name is Inocencia and she is my grandmother.

At first, when I refuse to eat, they attempt to tease me with ever more wondrous dishes. When this fails, as inevitably it does, they beseech me with scared, pleading eyes. Most especially my grandfather, Felix, who finally succumbs to tears.

'We have already lost the most treasured things in our lives, darling little Sofía. Our beautiful daughter Estelle and her beloved husband Bruno are gone from us forever. But now you are back to help heal our weary hearts. Please do this one little thing for us, please eat,' he mumbles through sniffs and snorts. 'This is all too much to bear.'

He rubs his bearded chin and sobs a little more and Inocencia wraps her arms around him and gently kisses the top of his grey pointy head. In the end I eat. Not for Felix, but because my growing stomach howls with pain. It has been a long time since breakfast. At home with Mama and Jordi.

I am to change my name it seems. Not my Christian one, but my family name. I am to become a Magdalena. According to Inocencia and Felix I have always been a Magdalena in spirit, from the day I was born. They talk of an abduction but I know they wish to poison my mind so I hum loudly above their words and drown out their malicious storytelling. Through my droning I hear them say that I share my 'mother's' features as well, and Felix scurries off somewhere to gather evidence. I hum louder still. I have to avoid their indoctrination at all costs. I have been warned.

Felix returns and I can see that they are both struggling with my hostility. I feel triumphant, for a few fleeting seconds, but my victory explodes into nothing as Felix shows me his evidence. Four framed photographs of my 'mother' and 'father', lain with such love and admiration before me from his shaking hands. I scream, wriggle and spit at them, lashing out as they attempt to appease me and I scratch some skin from Felix's puny arm in the process. I hate them. I hate them for showing my 'mother's' face to me so that I may recognise my own. And I hate her for giving me her nose and complexion and her habit of staring unfaltering into the eyes of others. I hate her for everything. I can barely withstand its brutality.

Eventually they take the pictures away, or turn them face down. And all is quiet again. I stop humming. I can see the pain in their eyes for I am not an insensitive girl, but I do not care. The anguish they cause me is far, far worse than that which I could ever inflict upon them. I am not a Magdalena and I never shall become one. It is my vow.

I do not have a brother now, but I do have four cousins and this is a new experience for me. Three boys and a girl, Josep, Rafael, Diego and little Ana. They are the children of my 'father's' brother, Bruno's niece and nephews, but it means nothing to me. With the exception of the girl, they are all older than I am and they treat me like a visiting queen. I am a precious gift from God once more and in a strange, hateful way I enjoy their attention.

Josep is the oldest at nineteen, ten years older than me. He smiles with the whole of his soft, brown face and speaks gently to me in a manner which I find intoxicating. I can see in an instant that there will be things which Josep can say to me that the others can not. He begins to say some of them today. And although I still protest just as vehemently as before when Josep talks of my 'mother' and 'father', I carry his words with me through the remainder of the day and mull them over and over in the quiet peace of the night.

I have my own room, a little down the passageway from Felix's and Inocencia's. One of the first things I do is consider my escape routes, but it would be hard to leave from the window. It opens well enough, I have checked already, but the drop is too high as the small garden below leans away from the house and the roof of the back porch is too far to reach. I will need to consider my options carefully. I hear Felix lock the front door and climb the creaky stairs heading for bed and I know that – for tonight at least – I am trapped here in this house with them.

I fight sleep but it arrives anyway. I am caught in a world of semi-dreams filled with strange men, exploding bombs and the face of my terrorist 'mother' smiling sweetly at me. Somewhere in the frantic mêlée, Josep holds my hand and tells me that everything will be alright. He tells me tales of when I lived in this house before, as a baby, before I was taken – along with my parents – on the road to the airport. Estelle and Bruno were fleeing to America, Josep tells me, for a life of freedom away from the military repression.

Even though there was little chance that they would have

been admitted to the US, they were determined to try and I drift through the hours of darkness dreaming of huge hamburgers, rows of billowing flags and tall, majestic skyscrapers. Everyone is smiling and happy but their faces rush past me in a frenetic blur. As I sleep it makes a jumbled sense but in the bright light of morning, I cry and cry. I hate them more now than ever before.

Soon after my arrival in the house, the letters begin to appear. Letters from home, from my mother and Jordi and even from uncle Carlos. I find them hard to read. Not in any physical sense, for their flowing writing is heart-stoppingly familiar to me. It is more that I cannot see them clearly through my tear-soaked eyes and I make many messy smudges upon their inky pages as the drops cascade to the paper.

It is on one such occasion, as I sit alone on the back porch of the silent house, that Inocencia sidles quietly up to me before I have the chance to flee. She creakily stoops beside me and sighs loudly, smiling kindly, 'So many letters,' she says, nodding at the pile in my lap. I say nothing.

'We wrote to you too,' she says, pulling the cord from a small sack which I only now see her carrying.

'Here,' she whispers, offering me a handful of the sack's contents. I do not move. I just stare at the sheaf of envelopes gripped within her wrinkled fist.

Inocencia sighs again and pulls her hand back. She stands awkwardly and smoothes out the crumpled letters upon a nearby table. It is now that I see she is crying. I'm sure that she has cried many times before but these are the first tears she has allowed me to witness. I should feel something. I should feel something other than anger and confusion.

Today is my birthday and I am going home. They say it is just a visit but I have great plans for an escape.

I have only been gone for four whole weeks but somehow my old street already looks different, with its twitching curtains and larger houses set back from the road. I feel nervous.

Mother and Jordi remain in the house, but it is difficult to pass quickly from the street into the safety of the parlour through the swarm of waiting journalists. I had not expected them to be here, to still be interested in my case. Inocencia says that I have become a 'cause célèbre' all around the city. It feels strangely good to be something so special, it sounds exotic. It sounds subversive. Inocencia knows many more extraordinary words than my mother.

We eat the cake which mother has baked especially for my tenth birthday and talk of unimportant things which hold little significance. Mother tells me of new happenings in the street and Jordi regales stories of school, with his usual humour and abandoned animation. She tells him to quieten down but I love his warmth. It is the only true thing left of my life in this house. Then it is time to go and I push my way back to the motor car, with its engine running. Ready.

I do not remember, until the evening lights of central Buenos Aires bounce upon my face, that today was the day I planned to escape. Maybe next time.

I am to restart school after Easter, as a Magdalena. There is little I can do to avoid the name change, but I shall try and try to ignore anyone calling me by it. There are three weeks to go until I return to the classroom and, in the meantime, I stay in the house. There seems to be no place for me in this topsy-turvy world but I find myself relaxing a little in the serenity of days spent with Inocencia. In these hours, I can feel the pressure on my chest lifting. I can almost breathe again.

Inocenia has stopped talking of my 'mother' and 'father'. She has not mentioned them in over a week now. Instead, we scrape and boil vegetables for Felix's dinner and strip and scrub the house for the almost daily deluge of cousins. I find great pleasure in the mundane familiarity of Inocencia's chores but that, I suspect, is her intention. She is very wise, this wrinkled old woman. Day after day, we work in silence but I know that one day, when she thinks me ready, she will once again talk of Estelle and Bruno. I begin to wonder what will be said.

'Hail Mary, full of grace, the Lord is with you. Blessed are you among women and blessed is the fruit of your womb. Holy Mary, mother of God, pray for us sinners now and at the hour of our death.'

Repeating the rosary brings a new found peace to my soul, one which I have not experienced for many months. Life at school is tough. It is not exotic being a 'cause célèbre' after all. It is not subversive. It is hard work.

It is now almost six months since I left home. I visit mother and Jordi every weekend but we are growing apart. It is difficult to know why. Except that is a lie. I do know why, it is because of the questions. Enriqueta pushes me now with such ferocity that I find myself willing away the hours spent in her house. She is convinced that Inocencia will turn me into either a thief or a terrorist.

I find myself defending the Magdalenas in a way I would rather not. And it confuses me to my very soul. Josep's words tumble and race around my head on days like this. I struggle with what to believe, but I no longer have difficulty with the obvious inaccuracy: Estelle was not a terrorist, she was just a student learning English. Josep has told me that her only 'crime' was to belong to the union, and I believe him, although I have never actually told him so. I almost believe him too when he tells me more of the plan she and Bruno had to escape with me to America, and that Estelle truly believed I had been handed back to Inocencia and Felix after her detention. I almost believe him, but not quite. I cannot quite bring myself to believe the horror.

What I do know for sure is that, in many ways, I would rather not visit Enriqueta and Jordi any more.

School has become a daily struggle. I would rather be invisible. I would rather be normal. I have missed too many classes to keep up and this adds significantly to my overwhelming conspicuousness. It could be much worse though, I suppose. I could be alone, but I am not. Josep has promised to help me when lessons finish during the summer months and I am painfully grateful for his kindness. I have only a few more months to wait. They are all being very kind. I have grown accustomed to writing Magdalena on my school books and answering the teachers when they call me. It is not so hard.

Josep works in a meat factory on the edge of the city. He is also in the trade union. He is not ashamed, but I am shocked. I have never known anyone in a union before and after the stories he has told me of Estelle and the animosity I remember my adoptive father held for such organisations, I am truly frightened for his safety. You may see that I say 'adoptive' now when I refer to my old family. It isn't that I have denounced them, it is merely that I find it helps to lessen the confusion. For others, and for myself.

As I tell Josep in hushed whispers that he must take great care, his eyes smile at me but his lips remain fixed. He is scared of belittling me, I can feel it.

'There is no need to worry so, little Sofía,' he says softly, taking my hand in his, 'those days have passed. We are free now to choose our own destinies. I am allowed to belong to the union if I wish, although I'm sure you are right that there are still those among us who would have it different. Don't fret so,' he adds, sensing my continuing disbelief, 'it is not as it was for your mother and father.'

I pull my hand away. I do not want to know about them. Or do I?

The cold of winter takes hold of this choking, noisy city. At weekends I am pleased to muddle through the mornings until the solitude and tranquillity of the siesta arrives. In a house of old people, it seems a winter siesta is as precious as its summer counterparts. With rooms swathed in silence, save for the frequent snoring of Inocencia and Felix, I often steal myself from sleep and take a book instead from the vast old bookcase. The back porch is deliciously chilled at this time of day. Mostly, I know not what I read, I simply marvel at the multitude of subjects and languages crammed into this tiny, revolutionary house.

But today, I do not read a book. I take Inocencia's letters instead. The first that I pull from the worn little sack is postmarked towards the end of 1983. Eighteen months ago. It is tatty and ripped and has obviously been well fingered, but never opened. It is addressed to Sofía Comorera. Me, with my old name. How strange it looks now. The address is roughly crossed through, several times with excessive force, and marked 'Not known here. Return to sender.' But the address is correct, it would have reached me. I have never seen this letter before today. She must have kept it from me, Enriqueta. I open it.

Half is from Felix and the other half from Inocencia. I recognise her jagged handwriting and his strange little capital letters. My grandfather writes of Estelle, her beauty and courage and her belief that the authorities had returned me to them. He knows she is dead. And from Inocencia I learn of the one unsettling telephone call from Estelle in prison and then the years spent hoping. Until the arrival of an anonymous photograph, several years later, showing me with another family. The photograph it seems changed their lives once again, restoring their faith that I was alive and beginning their long search to find me. There is much more to read but I refold the letter carefully and place it back in its envelope.

There are many, many more letters inside the sack. Some

half torn open, others with barely a mark upon them. Each one dated during 1983 and 1984, right up until the very week before I was brought here. Every single one returned to them without my knowledge. Inocencia and Felix wrote to me virtually every week for eighteen whole months.

There are other things here too. A child's reading book with the name Sofía Magdalena written elegantly across the front. In the hand of an adult. The writing is not mine, but the book obviously is. There is also a pair of faded pink shoes, tiny and well worn. I turn them over and over in my trembling hands and feel the tears cascading down my face. I remember them.

At the very bottom, I find the official court letter telling Inocencia and Felix that I am indeed their granddaughter. It contains the blood test result. Virtually 100% certain. I am a Magdalena.

And then there is the photograph. It is a bit blurred, as if taken at great speed by someone who dared not get too close. Perhaps it was one of those very same neighbours who stood beside the road watching me leave earlier this year. It is clearly a photograph taken in fear and subterfuge, but sent to Inocencia and Felix in truth and righteousness. It helped bring me back to them.

The photograph shows a petulant six-year-old being carried to a car by a severe-looking man. I gaze and gaze at the snapshot. At the instantly recognisable man. My adoptive father. Carrying me to his car. I think I can almost remember the day, but then there were numerous occasions when he took me to school in his shiny black car. Except now I know for sure that he wasn't my father and the uniform which I once thought so smart looks sinister upon his upright frame, with his face scowling angrily and his jaw set clenched. It is just a snapshot, I tell myself. A split second in time. He may well have laughed again the very next second. He wasn't angry with me, for he never shouted at his precious gift from God. Yet he was clearly annoyed with someone, as he bundled me into his shiny, black, unmarked police car.

I push the letters and assorted items back into the bag and throw it behind the couch. Angry tears burn down my face and I hate this world, this house, this family, with almost as much passion as I now love them.

Inocencia peels potatoes as though her very life depends upon it. The siesta has passed and the ravenous cousins will arrive for their Saturday meal in an hour or two. The back door is ajar with the coldest of afternoon breezes tickling in across our faces. And I ask her about my mother. My real mother. Estelle.

It is not far from this life to my old one, but I am never going back. I long for the lost promise of America and I plan to make the future better. I am a Magdalena.

Footnote:

Like the fictional characters of Estelle and Bruno, there are an estimated 30,000 men, women and children who remain 'disappeared' in Argentina as a result of the actions of the country's military regime between 1976–1983. Hundreds of babies and children were taken along with their parents and given to supporters of the government, whilst their mothers and fathers were incarcerated, often never to be seen again. Even today, these children are still being reintroduced and returned to their original families.

DONALD CAMERON
Writing Wrongs

I see the stares as I walk down the street, the gamut of emotions; some people, the braver ones, glare at me with outright hostility, others with disdain. Many, however, avoid my eyes and scurry on furtively, fear evident on their faces.

It wasn't always like this. Once I was one of them – the chattering classes, smug in their middle-income cocoons. Then, major worries included 'the falling value of mortgage endowments' or 'what time does the tapas bar start serving?' or 'why isn't this anti-fungal cream clearing my thrush?' and, especially common, 'why isn't little Nigel getting better marks at English? It must be his teacher!' Didn't the fact that 'little Nigel' couldn't be arsed learning the three primary auxiliary English verbs but could rhyme off the various capabilities and characteristics of all the vehicles in Super Mario Kart, spark a tiny ethereal glow in the low-wattage light bulbs of their brains?

Teaching seems like another life now. I see my face reflected in the street mirror of a shop window. Under my hat, the lines and shadows display an ordnance survey map of my life's sorrows, joys and fuck-ups. A youth gives me a V-sign behind my back to the delight of his colleagues. I turn slowly, not in the mood for confrontation: the group melts away into the crowd of shoppers, just another few corpuscles in the bloodstream of the city centre. No matter, I will remember them, wait for my opportunity. Many of my victims are cold cases, literally in the wrong place at the wrong time. On extreme occasions I may not act, preferring to feed on their fear and to bask in their gratitude, harvesting the sexual charge, rather than give them up to the machinations of the State. However, over time, I have become less fussy about the temperature of my dishes, so I never forget a face.

It seems a curious paradox that I, of all people, both as a former English tutor and now an unforgiving tool of an all-powerful autocracy, should have fallen foul of the power of the written word, having been damned forever by a tidal wave of propaganda.

Disillusionment didn't take long to occur in the modern state school, however keen I had been initially. The realisation that my pupils didn't share my enthusiasm for the works of Milton and were, as a rule, disinclined to share his joy in 'beholding the bright countenance of truth in the quiet, still air of delightful studies' gnawed away at me. The daily act of entering the classroom became a Promethean trial, the pecking and tearing being of my soul.

Now everything is so different, each day bringing new pleasures. Drunk with the intoxicating effect of my pen, I can hardly bring myself to sleep, so much do I savour my new existence, where my scribblings can alter lives. I want to feel this charge constantly, alert in my desire to punish, until the end of my days.

Last days . . . Yes, I remember well my last day as a teacher, travelling in on the underground, on an oppressively muggy day, my head pounding as I thought of the ordeal ahead – poetry appreciation with class 3D.

I entered the rowdy classroom determined to give it my best shot. Thinking, you never know, this day may be the day I touch something, in someone, remove the blinkers of modernity and reveal an old, different world, where words could be magical and not just blocks of letters to be shrunken and rearranged into text messages.

I talked of how poems had once been described as bridges built from the known, familiar side of life over into the unknown. Looking at the rows of bored faces, I could sense that no one was willing to accompany me on this particular journey. In fact, the foundations of this crossing were built on shifting sands of mistrust, which were about to be swept away by a strong wave of apathy. Approaching the end of the lesson, I followed the formulaic route of asking the class if anyone had any points to raise. Turning away I almost missed the slow rise of a pupil's hand. I was surprised to see the lumbering form of Nathan Graham stand up before me.

'Sir! Can I ask you something about the poetry stuff?'

A glimmer of hope fluttered within me, faint like a butterfly's wings on a maiden flight. I looked up at the swarthy, broad-shouldered pupil who, despite his youth, towered above me. It was a defining moment. Perhaps, just perhaps. I indicated for him to continue. He paused, looking about the class; inwardly I willed him on, yes, go for it . . . show me a spark to fan into a flickering flame . . . take your first step on to the bridge!

He breathed deeply, trying to gather courage. 'Sir,' he asked 'that poetry stuff . . . do you actually get paid to talk about that fuckin' shit?'

As laughter erupted around me, everything swam and I grabbed for the desk to steady myself. A chant began to echo round the room.

'Fuckin' shit . . . fuckin' shit . . . fuckin shit . . .'

I remember very little afterwards: flashbacks of a blind rage, grappling, the tearing of cloth, shouts and screams; numbly looking down at my cut and bruised knuckles as I tried to recover my bearings in the police station; my unsympathetic lawyer almost nodding in agreement as the policewoman detailed the charges against me; fellow officers coming into the interview room to stare at me, like visitors to the reptile house. The words 'attempted murder' hardly registered at the time, though I'd have plenty of time for reflection later.

A puddle of water thrown up by a passing bus splashes my feet, jerking me back to the present. Looking down the quiet side street, I feel the familiar, exciting stirrings in the pit of my stomach. Although it is only late afternoon, the winter darkness is casting a murky shroud. I lick my upper lip, tasting the salt. A not unpleasant shiver runs over my body as I stand in a doorway. These are the best moments: the stalk, the thrill of the hunt. I watched her leave her car almost half an hour ago; now the street is getting quieter, people scurrying home like rats disturbed in a sewer. Timing is everything. If she doesn't return soon, I'll have her as I've had so many before. That sweet moment when I pounce, the mixture of panic and bewilderment on their faces . . . it can't be happening to them. They're all the same.

The build-up to my court appearance had been front page

news – the tabloids kept the pot boiling nicely with headlines such as 'Class War!', 'Grapple for the Teacher!' and, my own personal favourite, 'Teacher's Teenage Kicks!'. Initial support from colleagues began to dwindle in the face of a barrage of publicity branding me as the teacher from Hell. Any hopes of a favourable outcome were extinguished when Nathan Graham, no doubt shrewdly advised of the blossoming culture of compensation, turned up in court in a school uniform which would have made Little Lord Fauntleroy look butch. Mentally vowing never again to work with children or animals, I tried not to flinch as the judge, pontificating on his duty to protect society, sentenced me to three years. Headline: 'Bully Gets Detention!'

What's there to say about prison? Dirty, squalid, long periods of boredom punctuated by moments of extreme fear. Eleven months of my sentence spent in solitary, ostensibly at my request 'for my own protection'. My wife visited once, buoying up my spirits with the news that she was leaving me. She'd found someone new, someone normal . . .

On release from prison, I returned to an empty flat. My wife had not only taken herself out of my life but most of our possessions and furnishings. Visits to the local Job Centre proved fruitless. A benefits officer – his features a definition of Weltshmerz – being kind enough to inform me that my prospects of employment were 'as promising as a lapdancer's in a Taliban training camp'.

The noise of high heels clattering down the street! Lost in my reverie, I've failed to notice the woman returning to her car from the opposite direction. Angry at my inefficient stakeout, I set off down the street to try and cut her off.

She seems to sense my presence, her legs moving faster now, almost breaking into a jog. My erection strains against the cloth of my trousers as I wonder if she's wearing stockings. She's running now, mild panic showing on her face as I close in. I can't run however, it wouldn't look good to draw such obvious attention to myself. I realise I'm not going to make it as she hurries into her car. I get within five yards, hoping she'll stall, but the engine starts first time and she screeches away, glancing at me fearfully through the spray from her wheelspin. I smile at her ironically, never mind . . . another time . . . another place.

Alone in my flat, I began to drink . . . seriously, but my drinking had an unusual outcome. Unlike the standard morality tales of descent, hand in hand with Dionysus, into a cirrhotic hell, as alcohol encouraged my liver to atrophy in its own enzymes . . . my life was saved by a bottle of cheap wine.

One afternoon, sensing the impending arrival of alcohol withdrawal, I gathered enough loose change to visit a local off-licence. As I scanned the shelves for affordable yet drinkable wine, I was surprised to meet an old teaching acquaintance. After enquiring what I was doing nowadays, he had the pre-science to ignore my claims to be getting by. Explaining that, although they couldn't raise their heads above the parapet, some former colleagues had considerable sympathy for my plight, he pressed a note into my hand.

'My uncle's number.' He explained: 'I'll have a word with him, he may be able to use your talents.'

With nothing much to lose, after waiting a few days so I didn't show my desperation, I rang the number. Uncle, it turned out, had a position of authority in a rather shadowy government agency. He told me 'how he admired my courage . . . that he yearned for a return to old values . . . he had the perfect position for someone with my strength of character.' Intrigued, I arranged an appointment with him.

We met in the local park and, true to stereotype, Uncle was wearing a raincoat and carrying a battered briefcase. Apologising for the unusual rendezvous, he explained it was important that no one at his department, in view of my previous notoriety, could put a face to my name. He went on to detail my prospective duties. I would watch the public and be ready to point the finger if need be. I would be expected to write for my paymasters and in return I would be looked after. I was to become part of a group separate from, and feared by, normal society.

'You do realise,' he added. 'Once you go down this road, it's goodbye to the old life. Friends would be left behind?'

Not having a lot to lose in either area, I nodded.

He asked me to sign some documents, saying he'd do what was necessary to bury my criminal record. Adding that we probably wouldn't meet again, but that he'd keep an eye on my progress, he shook my hand and walked away.

That was it. In what was to become a classic case of poacher turned gamekeeper, I was accepted. Ostracised for my, admittedly, foolhardy defence of the glory of the written word, I had become an instrument of a much-hated authority . . . the power of my pen being absolute. What I didn't appreciate at the time was that I had, in essence, been given licence to roam the streets, enabling me to avenge myself many times over.

I hear the sound of voices – a family are coming down

the street, mother and father laden with bags and Christmas parcels. They are exhorting their teenage son, who is dawdling along behind, to hurry up. It won't matter now. I have them, there's no escape. I love doing families, especially with teenage sons.

The parents see me but, unlike some, the will to fight seems to drain from them. An air of resignation falls over them as the mother clutches her child to her. This is going to be so easy.

I walk casually towards their vehicle, to cut them off – things are happening almost in slow motion. Deliberately, almost with a conjurer's flourish, I reach into my bag. I write down the date, time and location on the preprinted form. Aware that timing is everything, I wait until they are within touching distance of their car and then I pounce, wrapping the vivid yellow notice round the windscreen wiper. They reach their car at that very moment, to see the words 'Fixed Penalty' leaping out at them. They stand rooted: the husband scowls at his wife; they both turn to scowl at their son. Blame and recrimination hang in the air – one less present in the stocking perhaps?

I turn away whistling softly to myself, Paradise regained, for the nineteenth time today. Already I'm on the lookout, ever vigilant for more victims, although technically my shift is now finished. Perhaps I'll do some unpaid overtime . . .

ANDY DRUMMOND

A Chronicle of the World: 1840–93

It was primarily the war of attrition between Paraguay and
Manchuria which kept the islanders in their isolation. The
ambitious Lopez dynasty led an independent Paraguay to
the shores of the Pacific and established one of the greatest
naval powers of the nineteenth century. Manchuria, having
concluded treaties with Russia, meanwhile turned its attention
to the Pacific trade. And so began in 1844 one of the most
bitter and devastating wars of the century. The effects on
world trade were far-reaching, for few ships dared to venture
into that part of the high seas which lie between the Cape of
Good Hope on the one hand and Cape Horn on the other.
It was this disruption which determined the fate of those who
had been abandoned on the desolate Island of Kerguelen in
the South Indian Ocean.

From the inheritance of my father I came into possession
of an old family Bible. Not our family Bible, for it seems that
my family never rose to one. But a Bible which my father
had received under heavily mysterious circumstances from a
lady of Fort William. Which lady had inherited it from her
mother, who, in her turn, had been presented with it by the
famous explorer William Bruce in 1901, after a particularly

cold winter he had spent in the meteorological station at the top of Ben Nevis. A note inside the front cover reads: 'This Bible was given in gratitude to William S. Bruce at Gough Island in the year 1893 by Mr James Finlay, late of the Island of Kerguelen.'

The Bible is remarkable not for its age and decrepitude, dishevelled though it is; large sections barely hang together by threads and glue. So tattered and worn indeed that much of the New Testament threatens to slip into the Apocrypha. The book is remarkable not for the printed words that lie within, for they conform strictly to the Authorised Version of King James, but rather for the handwritten notes which appear in the margins of some of the pages. In places, the marginalia are torn and so rubbed thin and erased as to be completely illegible. In other places, the ink used was of such poor quality – made probably from mosses and perhaps the bodily juices of fish or sea-birds – that it has faded entirely. But enough remains to reveal a history of injustices which should now be brought forth to the public attention.

Without further ado I will set forth these notes that you may judge for yourself. We turn first to the marginalia to the Book of Exodus, Chapter One, reading from Verse One:

'My name is James Lunn, minister to the parish of North Jura. What I set down here is a true history, which began in the year of Our Lord eighteen hundred and forty,' begins the commentary, in the neat and bold writing of a man of learning. 'Should the Lord preserve this Holy Book, then my history will serve to record the many wrongs we have suffered at the hands of the Godless.

'After several years of hunger in the village of Kenuachdrachd,

I made an arrangement with Captain George Harris, whom I met in Glasgow, for his ship to call at Lagg and to take my people to Van Diemen's Land. Many of that community and from other places in Jura had already gone, to America mostly, to seek out new lands and a living for their children. We had heard that Van Diemen's Land was a place of plenty, of high forests and of green meadows. Harris told me that Van Diemen's Land was a place where all my flock could live as Godly men, without the oppressive practices of landlords and factors. Many of my parish agreed that this is what we should do.

'There were about four dozen of us in all who boarded the big ship at Lagg on the second day of April in eighteen hundred and forty, and who sailed down the Sound, leaving the bald hills behind us for the last time. I remember that many a mother wept and many a grown man as well, as the last sight of Jura disappeared in the clouds.

'It was on the first day of this awful journey that I found Captain Harris to be a fearful and godless man. He roared at the children if he saw them on deck and he was brutal to the sailors. Many a time I remonstrated with him and we shouted at each other, over the treatment of both passengers and crew, Captain Harris red in the face and with bunched fists, myself white as a winding-cloth and arms waving. On one occasion Harris used his fist to end such an argument, and I had to retire below deck for three days to nurse my swollen face.

'I cannot tell exactly what route we travelled, for I am a poor sailor and navigator upon the sea; but it was southwards all the way, through storms and flat calm, and heat and rain, for days and nights together. The ship rolled and turned even in the slightest swell, and many of us lay sick under deck, where we were tossed together. During one storm, which lasted for three days, the floor was slimy with their sickness. Our oldest parishioner, William Finlay, died in that storm, wild on his bed until the very last, when he suddenly sat up shrieking, then passed over. He was slipped over the side on the following day, his body to the waves, his soul to God. Two babies also died on that forsaken day.

'After several weeks, we turned towards the east. I learned from some of the crew that the dark coastline which we could see dimly to the north was Africa. One morning, not long after this, I chanced upon Captain Harris. He had been drinking heavily and boasted to me that he would be a rich man after this journey was over, for he was to set up in trade in the China Seas, where, as he said, spices and slaves, rum and women were to be easily had. Such a confession shocked my sensibilities and I remonstrated with him, calling him down for his ungodliness. Harris was in no way moved by these words and laughed openly in my face. "Ungodly, Mr Lunn? I tell you, you are dealing with the most sinful man you will ever meet," he bawled, "For I have stolen this ship and no man will ever catch me for it!"

'It seemed that Harris had obtained the ship by some trick, pretending to hire it for a short trip, but changing its name and appearance on the high seas, shortly before picking up his passengers from Jura. The whole act had been planned for many months. I had been deceived and implicated in all of this, for Harris had waited for our contract to be signed before he stole the ship.

'Of course, I was horrified at this revelation, and mortified that the God-fearing men and women of Jura should be setting out for a new life on a ship which was captained by a shameless criminal, and I chastised Harris openly for it. But my words were like hailstones in summer – soon melted and leaving no trace upon the sinner Harris. Over the next few days, I endeavoured to make the sinner see the error of his ways. But the man was so obdurate that my words found no way into his soul.

'The winds and the seas in that part of the world were wild. A gale blew night and day and again into night and day, huge waves towered over us from the rear and lashed us, and those of us who could still move had to care for friends and parents and children who were moaning in their cots. I led prayers for our salvation, almost incessantly. It was therefore with great relief that one grey morning we saw land to the south of us, and found that Harris was directing his ship towards that land. Some way off, on the horizon, we could just make out the sails of two ships disappearing to the east. Which ships these were we did not know.

'It was by my calculation the twentieth day of July, and I called on my flock to rejoice that we had finally come through all our troubles, with the hand of the Lord laid upon us, and that we had reached Van Diemen's Land in health and safety. Although it was July, it was not a summer's day. I observed Captain Harris who seemed to me to have a mocking smile on his face.

'All those who could bestir themselves came up on deck to see our new land. In all truth, it looked desolate and bare, unwelcoming. There was a huge mountain covered in snow which lifted itself up into the clouds and out of our sight.

The coastline was rocky and waves crashed upon it. The cloud came down low from the mountains and obscured much of the land. After several hours, our ship tacked into a rocky inlet, where there was shelter. But there was not a tree, not a blade of grass to be seen. Wild birds swooped and dived, screaming like demons. An anchor was cast and we rode on the restless sea for a time.

'I was beset by doubts and took Harris to one side and began to argue with him. "This cannot be Van Diemen's Land, sir!" I exclaimed, pointing at the most barren cliffs and headlands I had ever laid eyes on. "This land is no better suited for human habitation than Garbh Reisa." Harris smiled cruelly: "Have you ever seen Van Diemen's Land, Mr Lunn?" Of course, he knew that I had never travelled so far and could only stay silent.

'It was not possible to land in that bay, which the sailors named Port Christmas, for a westerly gale was howling across the land from the sea beyond, preventing the ship from approaching the far beach. At around midday, therefore, Harris turned his ship south and eastwards again, and we sailed swiftly among rocks and reefs, with the land to the south vanishing between the mist and the spray. We sailed for about six hours, fearing at every moment to be cast upon the rocks and to perish. At one time we sailed down a fast channel between a monstrous headland and a rocky island. At the head of the land to our right was a mountain which appeared briefly through the clouds. We passed through other rocks on which the sea broke terrifyingly but the sailors were skilful. When night fell we found ourselves in a sound where the water seemed calmer.

'The ship lay at anchor all night, and in the morning we were told to get on the boats with all that we possessed. I protested again that this could not be Van Diemen's Land, but Harris said nothing to me. He was occupied in moving the people from the ship to one of his two small boats, and in seeing them safely to land. Since the wind was rising again, it was a dangerous business. Each time that I tried to speak to Harris, or to his first mate, I was brutally shouldered aside, and could get no answer. I was in the last boat to leave. As the sailors pushed away from the side of the ship, Harris leaned over the rail above us. "You are right, Mr Lunn!" he shouted to me, "This is not Van Diemen's Land! But I am sure you will make it into God's own land with your men of Jura!" With that, we pitched into the surf now mounting rapidly and headed for the shore. The sailors avoided our eyes, and none would reply to my desperate questions, until one, moved perhaps by pity, answered my pleas for some knowledge of where we were being landed. "This is the Island of Kerguelen, sir, the Island of Desolation some call it. You are still some weeks away from Van Diemen's Land. May God help you all!"

'And with that blessing we were cast upon the shore of our new home.'

Many pages were required to write down this small piece of history and you should understand that we have by now reached Exodus, Chapter Thirteen. It was scarcely appropriate that the Pharaoh should let the enslaved people go, just at the moment when the enslaved people were abandoned upon the Island of Kerguelen. Nevertheless it was so. Take the time to consult your atlases and globes and see where Tasmania lies and where Kerguelen and where the nearest port of civilisation is.

Mr Lunn continues:

'We were left on a land without trees, without beasts, without shelter, by a man who had stolen his ship and now proposed to make a fortune in the warm seas of China. But the eye of the Lord was upon us and His Vengeance came in a most strange circumstance. No sooner had we been put ashore amongst those wailing families and friends, than the small boat pushed out into the waves again and made for the ship. But the wind, which had been strong enough until then, rose of a sudden to a gale and worse; it twisted and turned and began to strike up the sea before us into monstrous waves. The ship was tossing at its anchor like a piece of wood. The small boat was snatched up, driven sideways into some rocks and was smashed into a hundred pieces before our eyes. What became of the sailors we could not see, for the rain and the foam lashed into our faces and we had to seek shelter. And then the great thing happened!

'The Very Great Vengeance of the Lord Almighty came down upon the Devil in flesh, George Harris. For the wind blew stronger yet and waves like hills rose up and crashed upon the ship and tore it from its anchor and sent it hurling across the sound towards the rocks! Oh! as we stood on the shore we knew that the Good Lord was with us, and I led my people in psalms to thank Him for these acts. And as we sang, Harris and those of his crew who could, leaped from their ship like the souls of the damned into the Pit, and they plunged into the foaming torrent and disappeared from our sight.

'Oh! the ways of the Lord are mysterious but glorious to behold!

'No sooner had the Lord God emptied that ship of its heartless and sinful crew, than He bade the storms be silent and the waves be still, and a fresh breeze to come in the stead of the great wind. And as Harris and his men pulled themselves out of the water on the shore of a small island out there in the sound, their ship, now purged of sin and grief, set its own sails and sailed peacefully out to the open sea and at a steady speed towards the east.

'The God-fearing souls of Jura were left on the main part of the land, and the sinner Harris and some of his crew on their island, the two tribes separated by a sea in which the currents flowed fast. And never a boat for either of us. As the storm died away and the ship which had been our home disappeared fast behind a headland, I led a prayer of thanksgiving and then we left the shore in search of a place to build shelters.' Here is a curious thing: the Reverend Lunn continued his account of those terrible events only at Joshua, Chapter Twenty-Two. This lacuna was not of the physical sort, the ravages of time having eaten away at memories: there was simply no writing of any sort in the margins of the remainder of Exodus, nor yet in Leviticus nor in Numbers.

'We found very little shelter but, at some distance from where we had been landed, and protected behind a small hill, a place which we thought might suit to build some huts. And in the first few days that we were there, we built with our bare hands, digging rocks from the very hillside, collecting turfs and seaweed to fill the gaps as best we could. But how many times did we build up only to have a wind knock it down. In those first few days and nights, with a gale blowing without end, and the rain coming down upon us as upon Noah, we lost several small children and two old men who died in the night, with only my poor words of ministration to comfort them.'

And again there is a great gap, for Mr Lunn had chosen to continue his story in the Book of Job:

'When we had built enough shelters from the rocks and stones and had filled the cracks with moss, and had buried those who had died of exhaustion and starvation and fever, we began to arrange our lives. There was no wood which we could use for fires, but peat and seaweed aplenty. It became possible to cut and dry peat, using our bare hands for the most part, since we had few tools with us.

'For food, we set out at the break of each day, men and women and children, to hunt down seals or birds or anything that had wings or scales or fur. After a whole day, it was possible to return home with nothing to show for the hunt. But we learned where the auks and the fulmar and the petrel were. Seals were not easily found and less easily killed. We all joined in, from the youngest child to the oldest woman, for only thus could we find enough to feed us and keep us from day to day. I accompanied these parties if there was no sick person to tend to. Always one or two of the old people were left behind at our shelters to tend the fires and cut more peats.

'It seemed that we had arrived in the worst days of winter. I tried to explain that the Southern hemisphere had opposed seasons to the Northern but I do not think many really understood. It was July when we left the ship, and in Jura the skies would have been calm and the days warm. Down here, the clouds raced without end, the days were short and the nights full of wind and sleet and snow.

'After fifty days, the nights grew shorter and we saw the sun in brief moments. A more optimistic man than I might have named it Spring. And then a thing happened which would have saved us all had it gone well. A ship appeared in the sound and a small boat was put out. We all watched from the shore, as the boat was rowed out to the island on which Harris and his remaining crew had been wrecked. We knew these men to be still alive, for we saw every day small figures moving about. We watched as the boat landed and then pulled away again, with several more men aboard. When the boat had visited the ship again, there was a delay of an hour or more, which we did not understand. I waved my arms furiously to attract some attention and our best men shouted and the women wailed. To no avail, it seemed.

'At last, the boat put out again, with two or three men standing in it, armed with long guns. It came close to the shore but did not land. I called out to them to come ashore and to save us all from certain death. There was a man in the boat, with long fair hair, who spoke few words of English. It seemed they were hunters after the whale, from Norway.

'"I will not land," shouted the man in the boat.

'"For the love of God, man," I cried, "Can you not take away at least our poor children?"

'"No, sir," said the other, "For if you have the plague, I will not land."

'"The plague?" I shouted, "We do not have the plague. Please come ashore and see for yourself."

'"I am sorry, sir. Mr Harris has told us your story," answered the sailor, "And I cannot put my ship at risk. We will ask another ship to come later in the year."

'And with that, the boat put about and the ship left into the east, with the devil Harris and his men on board, never to be seen again.'

'Already we had lost about ten of the forty souls who had landed – babies for the most part, and old men. We buried them as we could in shallow graves and marked the graves with stones. And still we carried on. I, who had been a fit man full of hope when we had left Jura, felt that I had aged beyond my years, my hair now almost white and with a long white beard. I tried to speak to my people with the words of comfort and of judgement from the Bible in which I now write and which was our only book of wisdom. But even I, in those months, sometimes wondered aloud to my friends whether the Good Lord had deserted us in our hour of need. I read much in the Book of Job.

'During our summer, we found that a cabbage which grew in profusion did much to keep us alive, for it seemed to keep our eyesight sound and our skin healthy. The cabbage and the oily flesh of the birds, and their eggs – such was our food in that year and in all the years to come. But it did not close our doors to death nor to sickness nor to despair.

'In the second Spring on that island, I asked several of the younger men to go on a journey into the island, to see what they might find in the hills behind us. We had until then walked for many miles along the shoreline, both east and west, in search of food, and had found other places where we might live. No one place was any better than others. Water was to be found everywhere, as were the birds, the cabbage and the seals. Some glens were more sheltered than others, but none exceeded the benefits of our first place of landing.

'It was a morning of fog on which five young men set off. What a journey that must have been! They were away from their families for twenty days and nights, and they saw many lochs and many bays and rocky shores to the south, and places where fishing might be good. They saw long, long hills abandoned by God. They saw bogs stretching to the horizon, over which they stumbled for hours, as in a slough. They saw distant mountains rising with snow on them from behind hills which they knew they could not climb. They saw a coastline which was far, far longer than all of the shores and hills of Jura put together many times. But they saw not one other living soul, not one creature of the land and not one man.'

We have to turn to the three Books of Nahum, Habbakuk and Zephaniah for the next legible entries. In the Books of Isaiah and Jeremiah, many of the pages have notes which are now illegible. The writing in the later Books was not that of Mr Lunn: it was far less confident, larger, the words encroaching upon the printed text, with an abundance of ink blotches and extraordinarily poor spelling and grammar (which I have here corrected, for it would be a shame to spoil my own good prose with these ill-educated words). I suppose this had been the work of another of the poor exiles.

'The whalers came back in the third year after our arrival. A ship put down its anchor and a boat came out to our shore. This was the Year of the Doctor, for there was a learned doctor on the ship. Having no English, he made himself understood to Mr Lunn by signing and drawing on a slate. He seemed surprised that we had not all died of the plague which Harris had said had afflicted us. He was able to treat some of our worst sicknesses. Mr Lunn asked if the ship could take some of our people off the island. The surgeon told him that this was not possible. The ship was on a hunting trip that would last two years, and could take no passengers, nor yet even a letter.

'But the Norwegian was most interested in our cabbage. He took as many as we could give him. He gave in return some bits of wood, nails and tools and two bags of grain which could be spared. He also promised to return on a future voyage and trade with us again.

'I believe that the sailing away of this ship broke Mr Lunn's heart, for he took to his bed and died soon afterwards. Thomas Finlay took the Bible to himself and read to us from the Book every night and twice on the Sabbath.

'Another two years passed and in the Year of Grey Snow another whaling ship called. It was Norwegian. The captain seemed to have knowledge of us. He came ashore and was warmly greeted. He brought wood and grain with him, which was most useful to us. He traded for cabbage and for salted eggs.

'Captain Sorensen told us of the war raging between Paraguay and Manchuria whose ships were now greatly feared. There were pirates upon the high seas and no man was safe from them. The captain told us that we had best to remain quietly where no one should think to discover us. When he told us these things, we were glad that we were apart from the sinful world. We were untouched by war and pirates, safe in the hands of the Good Lord. Captain Sorensen promised to return again in the following year, if he were spared. He would take us off if the wars had finished or trade with us again if the wars continued.

'In the Year of the Stranded Whales, another ship came. It was from Boston in America and the captain brought bad tidings. The war between Paraguay and Manchuria still prevented him from taking us off the island. He brought worse news too. On the first day of eighteen hundred and forty-seven a great storm of huge fiery bodies fell from the stars upon the sea between Scotland and America. The waters between Zetland and Iceland were boiled away. Dry land was revealed upon which a man could walk for many leagues. A huge wave was set up which crashed upon Scotland and split the whole land apart between Fort William and Inverness. The north of the land was sundered from the south of the land and a vast gulf lay now between them. The waves which had caused this devastation carried on to the lands of Europe and swept away Amsterdam and Berlin and Paris and Rome. Little was left of the great lands there, nor yet of the many sinners of Paris of whom the captain had heard tell.

'The captain told us that the world was an evil place and that we should stay here for the moment. If God spared him he would return in two years to take us off. In the meantime our friends thanked us for our cabbage and our salted sea-birds. They left us some sacks of grain and many spars of wood with which we repaired our houses. Many among us wished that the seas between our island and Van Diemen's Land would

dry up like the story of the Red Sea. We would walk from
here to a better place.'

In the Book of Zechariah, yet another hand is evident:

'In the year which followed the Year of Hunger, we were
visited by a ship. It was from Russia. The captain spoke little
English. But we managed to trade news for cabbage and
eggs. We discovered that this ship was fleeing from great
devastation. The rebels of Finland had in that year invaded
the lands of Russia and Prussia and Denmark. They killed
the kings and emperors of these lands. They subjected their
peoples to grievous taxes and outrages. The captain said that
the Finlanders would cause a war in all of Europe. He advised
us to stay in peace and isolation. He promised never to tell
his enemies of our island. He departed on his long journey
in search of the whale.'

The last legible entry recorded in this Bible lies at the end
of the Book of Malachi, where the Lord remonstrates against
those who have used harsh words against Him. The hand of
the chronicler is very poor and the fragment is short:

'There are two of us. John Finlay is the brother of my
mother. I am James Finlay. Many years have passed since we
came to this land. I was born here five and forty years past.
We are told that all the world is consumed by fire and water
and the Angels of God have visited wrath upon all men. We
alone live on. Few ships come to visit us now for the whale
is also gone.'

And with that final entry terminates the history of the
people of Jura exiled upon Kerguelen and held captive there
by world events beyond their control.

ROBERT ALLAN FREEMAN

First Love

Spring, my love, and I must leave,
And when the autumn comes, don't grieve.
For I am buried far away,
And bright green leaves
Grow from this clay.

Otto Wolfarth, March 1944 (fragment)

Spring! Unless one has lived upon this landscape it is difficult
to imagine the feelings this evokes. It's not the spring of home,
where the slumbering trees wake to dazzle us with their vibrant
green visions.

Here, the winter is far better. Winter, at least, is an enemy
we can relate to. It keeps us busy; warming the engines,
foraging wood, breaking holes in the latrines, staying alive.
But when the spring comes the endless steppe unwinds – a
truly hopeless place. The melancholy of its endless horizons
enters our souls and eats away our humanity.

'Lebensraum!' The word makes us smile. There's more than
enough of it here for all of us. Too much for many of us. And
for some of us, all there will ever be! To make good these

losses they send us more men; younger and more bewildered with each new draft.

He turned up on a moody day in early spring; snow and ice melting. The few tracks through the Pripet Marshes were reverting to slush and the countryside was beginning to reveal its endless monotony. For obvious reasons he'd avoided the first draft. Twelve months later though, things were different. He was just a fortnight past his nineteenth birthday when Bernt Schenke joined the assault gun company.

There was a time we'd be curious. Scrutinising each new face. Assessing. Appraising. But not any more. We were more eager now to study the replacement half-tracks. They would be useful. Necessary. We listened to the note of the engines. Steady, throaty, powerful. We'd be needing them. We were moving back steadily. Not that it seemed to make much difference, the steppe just swallowed us up. Forwards and backwards were no longer concepts with any meaning.

As we meddled with the engines they came trudging past: a long, grey line of anxiety. Schenke alone was smiling. Inquisitive. His incredulous, wide blue eyes darted everywhere, but the smile marked him out. Slack jaw, the lips hanging wide, a parody of a smile.

Kentze nudged an elbow in my ribs, pointing him out, 'Look at that!' A kind of resigned humour in his voice. 'It's all up now . . . They're sending us the village idiots!'

'At least you can see he's an idiot.' I said. 'Who'd think it to look at you?'

The blow which followed that remark, though friendly, still managed to loosen a tooth. I nursed that tooth for days. Unwilling to let go. All through the relentless orchestra of noise that played on, day after day, outgoing – incoming, until the brain, pummelled by the endless concussion of the guns, and the hollow fear of the Russian counter-batteries, lapsed into a kind of absence. A paradoxical resignation. I was convinced if I could save that tooth I, in turn, would be saved.

*　　*　　*

> *The shadows lengthen, earth is fey,*
> *Beneath Her mantle, silver grey.*

Otto Wolfarth, April 1944 (fragment)

We moved again. Struggling the guns out of the mud into which they had driven themselves deeper at every discharge.

Sweaty, cursing work. Yet I never heard Schenke once complain. He wasn't strong, he wasn't even willing, just uncomplaining. A good soldier never questions an order. That made Schenke better than good – he didn't have the wit to question. He just carried on regardless and we envied him that.

Soon, after a fortnight in which he'd managed to stay alive, he earned the nickname of 'Professor'. Derisory, yes, but Schenke wasn't as stupid as he looked. He knew he'd been accepted and now he'd laugh along with us when we tormented him. He acted up to the role – and that was his undoing.

Again we moved. This time, at night, again westwards, perhaps eight or twelve kilometers. As the early dawn unfolded we took up positions around an abandoned farmstead. No more sleeping under tarpaulins, at least not for a while. Now we had a barn, and the abandoned farm buildings. Best of all, the nearby hamlet still supported a meagre population. We could scrounge, beg, or if it came to it, simply take a share of their few remaining luxuries. There were, we noticed, a few thin chickens scratching around in the dirt.

Old women, old men and a few children watched us trundle past. Grimy, indifferent faces – no strangers to oppression – they watched us with a cynical gaze. Men and women with stooped, weary shoulders, their children with opaque, lustreless eyes. Life was a torment, which no longer held either terror or surprise.

Yet these were the same people who, in a different lifetime, had welcomed us with flowers, as liberators from this oppression. They either knew better now, and realised there was little to choose between us and the Bolsheviks, or else feared reprisals more than they feared us. We, on the other hand, felt a gladness. Like the end of a pilgrimage. We had returned to society. Mean, Spartan and grudging, but society nevertheless.

We settled ourselves in, dug slit trenches, emplaced the guns, wired our defences and waited. Nothing happened. For days, nothing happened. Ivan had either shot his bolt, or else he was preparing something nasty. Either way, he was quiet for now.

He was still quiet when he sent one of those probing, desultory shells across. Just to let us know he was still there. It burst on the gable end of the farm. A large lump of masonry hit Lanner, our NCO. It took him squarely on the back of the head: he was dead before he hit the ground.

That's the trouble with these calms. One becomes complacent: ambling about, listening to the bird song and the voice of the wind in the branches, and marvelling how the leaves reflect the sunlight in shivering cascades, like twinkling jewels.

How quickly normality returns. Lanner didn't deserve it. He looked after us as if we were the children he was always talking about. He worried to death about them. One, Karl, was reasonably safe, an internee, but the other, Jurgens, was in the navy. He worried about him. I think he worried about us in the same way.

Not so his replacement, Stürmbahnführer Nette. We were curious about him, as we watched him climb from the truck three days later. The black uniform was ominous. We'd heard how the ranks were being 'stiffened' with these SS men. Discipline and morale were under strain; their job was to see we kept steady, else a bullet in the back of the head!

He was a thoroughly odious creature. We found out he was one of those low-life thugs who had joined the Party to avoid trouble with the law. He revelled in his field command; saw it, in some oblique way, as a reward. And he used it to practise a brand of sadism synonymous with the aristocratic Prussian military, though he himself came from the slums of Hamburg.

From the very beginning he had it in for Schenke. Whether he viewed him as the most expendable or the most vulnerable is a question open to charity, but he made his life hell.

The dirtiest, most dangerous jobs always went to Schenke. And where Lanner had mollycoddled him, Nette reviled him. The smallest misdemeanour brought down a tirade of fury. How things can change in the space of a week.

'You're pig stupid!' he was bawling: Schenke, still smiling, simply agreed.

'Yes, sir, pig stupid.'

This must have inflamed Nette, for the next thing out comes his PPK and he's pushed the barrel into Schenke's mouth. 'You're a disgrace to the Reich! There's a place for trash like you!' He was screaming at him, face red with rage and excitement. He'd even cocked the hammer of his gun.

We thought he was going to do it! He could have. But he saw us watching, and perhaps thought better of it. 'Bullets are for the Russians . . . too scarce for freaks like you!' He extracted the pistol and spat full in his face instead. Schenke was trembling from head to foot. His blue eyes darted in all directions; his jaw was slack, his lips hung wide in terror. With Nette on the prowl, who needed Russians?

*　　*　　*

And you are like the East Wind,
Whose soft and gentle tears,
She cries at night,
For some respite,
To all of mankind's fears.

Otto Wolfarth, April 1944 (fragment)

We'd always despised the Russians, but I realised then that it was men like Nette who were the real enemies. The pompously self-important, the bullies, the sadists, the psychopaths. I was not alone in this realisation. From then on a new wariness enveloped us all. Nette certainly sensed it, not that this checked his depravity, but he became withdrawn, suspicious, and avoided even the scanty social contact he'd enjoyed up until then. But, if only we'd known it, it was upon Schenke that the most profound change fell. He was terrified of Nette now. He lacked the vocabulary to explain this to us but, worse still, he lacked the understanding to explain it to himself. The concept of hate was so utterly alien to him, that the shock of it set up a resonance within him that became physically apparent whenever Nette appeared. But at least Ivan was still quiet. The big push he'd threatened still hadn't materialised. There wasn't much to do except think, and in the evenings get drunk.

One such evening Nette joined us. He normally kept his distance, he sensed the ill-will. But this night, either bravado or loneliness got the better of him, and he came across to our billet. He was already drunk. He brought with him, perhaps as a peace offering, five bottles of French brandy. Where he'd got these from we couldn't even guess. But it made a welcome change from the fiery vodka. Soon we were all flushed and merry. As usual, Rath was talking about women: the soft, perfumed sirens who inhabited our imaginations.

'Remember that girl in Aux-Chappel, with the tits as big as Goering's arse!'

'Do I!'

'Is there anybody who doesn't! I'll bet the entire company went down that road!'

'That explains a few things!' said Kentze, making a show of scratching his privates.

Schenke, as usual, was uneasy with this talk. All the more so, because Nette was with us. It was striking too, that he no longer smiled whenever Nette was about. A fact not lost on Nette.

'What's up Schenke?' he leered. 'Don't you know what

we're talking about? Haven't you ever skewered a sow with that useless piece of pig-meat? Or do you just think about it, when everyone else's asleep?'

Schenke mumbled an answer to the table top, 'Never had much luck with girls.'

Nette bounced a fist off the table, 'A virgin!' He roared, 'We can't have that. This is a rough, tough company . . . you're letting the side down boy!' He was laughing, but not in the roguish manner of a comrade, his laughter was the self-satisfied gloating of the bully. An ugly atmosphere evolved and as it spread Nette's face became contorted by the thought of an even uglier idea.

He buttoned his tunic, checked the chamber of his PPK, straightened his cap and walked to the door. 'I'll be back soon' was all he said.

'So what's all that about?' said Kentze, as soon as the door had banged shut behind him. 'What d'you think the big arse-wipe's got on his mind now?'

Schenke began to tremble again. Nette unnerved him at the best of times, but now something was cooking, that was for sure!

'I think I'll turn in' was all he said, but we could see he was in a funk.

'Stay and have another drink!' said Rath, 'Don't let that shit-heap get you down, we'll look after you. He'll get what's coming to him, one way or another.' Rath must've been drunk as he would never have said that normally, no matter what he really thought.

But Schenke couldn't be consoled: Nette was up to something and all he wanted to do was get into his bunk and hide.

We just shrugged, 'O.K.' and carried on.

By the time Nette returned, the six of us had seen off the brandy, and we were in musical mood. But the singing stopped abruptly when we saw what Nette had been up to. He had hold of the woman by the scruff of her neck, the PPK pressed hard against her hair. At first sight we were reminded of those thin chickens.

His face was even redder than usual: hers was ashen. He was panting with excitement. She must have thought she was here to be shot. Her lips were mumbling out what I imagined was a prayer. But we knew he wasn't going to shoot her, at least not yet. But in God's name, how low could a man sink?

She was probably in her early sixties, but deprivation had added ten years to her appearance. She was skin and bone, wrapped in rags, with distant grey eyes, moist with tears.

'Where's the virgin!' bawled Nette.

No-one replied, we were dumbstruck with amazement. By now the woman had peed herself with fright. Rath started to laugh; he really found this funny. He laughed till he choked for breath and tears rolled down his cheeks. Nette ignored him.

'I'll find him! Come on whore!' And he began to drag her towards the door that led to our bunks. 'Three volunteers . . . to assist with training!' He screamed these words at us, but no-one moved a muscle, except Rath, whose shoulders were still heaving.

Only the woman flinched as the pistol detonated. The bullet flew harmlessly upward.

'That's an order!' he screeched. 'All of you!'

We thought he'd really lost it. We weren't going to risk a bullet for the sake of the old peasant. Nette was irrational at the best of times but this was no longer a joke. Schenke must have heard the pistol shot and the shouting. He was lying under his blanket, blubbering, when Nette burst in and threw the woman on top of him. Both of them lay there, shaking with terror.

'Sorry I couldn't find a virgin for you!' His fat face was creased by a lurid grin. 'Come on Schenke, don't be embarrassed, she's seen it all before!' He was laughing like a maniac now, enjoying his own joke, but nothing was happening. Schenke and the old woman were both rigid in shock.

'Come on, Schenke, give her that pig-sticker you keep inside your filthy trousers!'

The pistol thundered again. It was unbelievably loud in the confined hut. 'That's an order, Schenke! The next one goes through you both!'

The woman was wise. He would have shot them both. She understood, at last, just what was happening to her, and she intended to survive. It was sickening to watch. In one way we should have felt privileged. We were probably the only ones in the entire army to witness a peasant raping a soldier. But it wasn't pleasant. We looked on with stony faces. Schenke and the woman were trembling and crying, making a bad job of a bad job; only Nette enjoyed the spectacle. When it was over she wrapped her thin clothes around herself, stood up, and without a glance left or right, walked through us and out of the door. That saved her. If she had just lain there, like Schenke, whimpering and snivelling, Nette would have been forced to do something with her. I think she sensed this and I admired her nerve.

As soon as she'd passed through the door Kentze distracted

the monster, who surely had it in his mind to kill her once his joke had been played out.

'Filthy bastard Schenke! She could've been your grand-mother!' He spat the words out with real venom. Then I understood.

'Yes Schenke,' I said, 'you're a pervert, you ought to be court-martialled. Filthy pig!'

Nette couldn't resist – he came out with such a tirade of filth I swear he never drew breath for a full five minutes; by which time the woman had vanished into the night.

Whether it was a result of this outrage, or whether it was just another inevitable horror, I wouldn't like to say but shortly afterwards we found ourselves on the receiving end.

The nights were misty now. We were close to the marshes – ideal cover for the partisans who flitted in and out of our lines with perfect impunity. It was two days later when we woke to discover a gruesome sight, which soon banished all thoughts of sympathy for poor Schenke.

Tied together with string, and nailed to the door of the barn, like a string of sausages, were the genitals of three of our men. We knew they were our men, we found their bodies later that day. Tied in a circle around a tree, their mouths gagged, their trousers open, and no sign of a merciful bullet, the bastards must have watched them bleed to death.

Inevitably, the order came down to take reprisals. I imagine Nette must have done some arse-licking, since our company got the job, when it should have gone to Wemeyer's unit; after all, they were his men. But Nette wasn't about to let the opportunity pass and Weymeyer wasn't going to object.

After a while one becomes numb to horror, yet the thought

of taking reprisals just seemed so pointless. But orders are orders. Nette was revelling at the idea though. He made an attempt at oratory – pathetic, lofty words which did little to disguise his sadistic impulses. Then he marched us off towards the hamlet.

The peasants were obviously unaware of the night's events; none made any attempt to hide or run away. Some argued, others wanted to collect belongings. An old man stood outside his house clutching an accordion. Nette dashed it from his hands and stamped the bellows flat: 'You won't be needing that where you're going, shit face!'

We rounded up as many as we could find of the old men, old women and the few children. Only now, of course, it wasn't indifference that stared back at us. We kept them at the end of our rifles while a makeshift jib was erected. Then they were forced to watch as three of us teased off the stars from lengths of barbed wire. There was no rope! And the barbs would interfere.

All this time Nette marched up and down, haranguing them, waving his PPK in their faces. We tried not to look, concentrating on the sharp stars, as though we could somehow distance ourselves from it all. Then I noticed Schenke. He was smiling. Not in his usual absent, airy way, he was smiling at something in particular. I followed his gaze, and there, among the ragged ranks of the condemned, the old woman was smiling back. They seemed to have forged a bond during that awful interregnum. Both had been victims of the same evil. Nette merely personified it. That smile was a tangible bridge between them, across which the woman seemed to pass all of her life's instruction. It was uncanny, this was the first time

I had seen Schenke look thoughtful. I was surprised to see it. But what really raised the hairs on the back of my neck was the woman. She wore such an expression of compassion, one would think the roles were reversed. I think she felt sorry for Schenke, because he was young and stupid, and above all innocent, and she knew that he, at least, would carry the image of what was about to happen until it filled the emptiness of his mind, until it burgeoned, like a tumour, and pounded at the walls of his skull. Soon, she would be released; he, on the other hand, would never again be free.

Nette had also noticed.

I don't know what gave him the most pleasure, kicking the woods from beneath the terrified peasants' feet and listening to their gurgling songs of death, or forcing Schenke to do it, when it came to the woman's turn.

* * *

There the cool water ripples
Among the apple branches.
And the roses' shade lies everywhere.
And from the quivering leaves
Floats down oblivion

Sappho, 580 BC (fragment)

When it was all over and done, and we were on our return, Nette came alongside Schenke, and began taunting him.

'Did you love her? The old peasant woman?'

Schenke didn't pay much attention. He had a picture in his mind which pounded at the walls of his skull. It wouldn't come out. He knew he would never be free!

The bright images that once flashed across his awareness and mapped out his world seemed to be condensing as if some chemical catalyst had been added. As if a photograph was gradually taking shape and depth and meaning. He woke from a dream into a nightmare. Now the image was frozen, detailed. He could walk around it, study it.

The shoes tantalisingly close to the ground, toes pointed in a last desperate, futile stretch. The threadbare garments. The puffed faces, the eyes. The bitter embrace of the wire, and the excrement running down their legs. The image took root, blossomed. He saw a fly enter a man's ear.

'Wrong! Wrong! Wrong! Monster! Monster! Monster!' He was suddenly conscious. Nette was just a wobbling, disincarnate, pink face, obscuring the pendulous string of corpses. He was mouthing obscenities.

It happened so fast then that the first we knew was Nette, on all fours, whimpering, pleading, and Schenke, the PPK in his hands, sobbing, gusts of tears rolling down his face. A dark stain had appeared on the crotch of Nette's precise, black uniform. His face was pressed into the earth, his arms thrown over his head. Schenke was screaming at him, 'Monster! Monster! Monster!' We watched, dumbstruck, as Schenke cocked the hammer, and before we realised his true intention, he'd pushed the barrel deep inside his own mouth, and pulled the trigger. The image was gone!

The last I remember of his face were his wide, blue eyes –
no longer incredulous.

Postscript

*Otto Wolfarth was reported 'missing in action' on 15 February
1945. The above cited fragments of poetry, together with his diary
(upon which this story is based) were unearthed by a Polish labourer
in 1987, near the town of Grunberg, in Northern Silesia. They are
all that remains of his memory. Unlike these fragments, his body
lies as yet undiscovered. The message of his poetry is unclear, the
message of his diary unheeded. He was twenty-seven years old.*

*The 10th Panzer Division (Frundberg) with which he served,
finally surrendered to the Allied XX Corps less than three months
later in Saxony, on 4 May 1945.*

GRISELDA GORDON
Ayurveda

Mr Abdullah, the owner, and his Danish wife are on the doorstep to greet the Macrae family as they arrive. The guesthouse is not quite as described in their well-thumbed guidebook. *Tucked neatly into the hillside above Kandy, the Nirvana Inn boasts magnificent views of the lake and the Temple of the Tooth.* From the rooftop maybe, Mrs Macrae thinks. Only then might one catch a glimpse of the grey silken water, which she remembers so well.

Mrs Macrae is nevertheless glad of her choice. She wants her family to experience a humble, local establishment, somewhere altogether earthier than a large resort hotel. She yearns to show them the essence of her life then.

Their room on the second floor is spacious and clean, and while there is no sign of the lake, the balcony affords an excellent view of the guesthouse garden. Everywhere fecund greenery steams and heaves with moisture: hibiscus bushes froth with pink bloom; a Na tree in the corner, provides shade to a visiting dog; thorny yellow bougainvillea entwines itself through the balcony railings. The shrill ring of birdsong. The smell of damp earth rising. It is the start of the rainy season.

At dinner they sit around a table covered with a red-checked cloth, hungry and tired after their long journey. The night air is damp and still. The heat has taken its toll on their three children – Alastair, Eilidh and Fiona – who loll over their chairs like rag dolls. Mr Macrae cracks open a bottle of beer. Mrs Macrae stares into space, a battered journal lying open next to her. Mosquitoes dive-bomb around their ears.

Mrs Abdullah appears from the kitchen with dinner. Large steel platters of steaming curries are placed on a long lace-covered table: bright green mung bean dhal; hotly spiced, pickled aubergines; ash plantain curry; coconut sambols; a yellow curry of dried fish, and Mallung, a dish of shredded and stir-fried greens. Mrs Macrae is surprised to hear Mrs Abdullah speaking Singhalese with Nifal the cook, a wiry Tamil from the hill country. Mrs Macrae was once able to talk as fluently as that. A few scattered phrases and odd fragments are all she can resurrect now.

Their fellow guests are all British, mostly travelling couples in their forties. They all clutch the same guide as her own, the green one with the masked dancer on the front. Perhaps they have chosen the Nirvana Inn for the same reason: its glowing reference and the emphasis on 'clean'. Ethnic, but undeniably safe. She goes to the buffet and piles her plate high. She feels suddenly far removed from the girl in Punjabi pants, silver anklets and frizzed up hair who arrived here twenty years ago, a gap student with a whole new world at her feet. Where was that free spirit now?

As they eat, Mrs Macrae glances over at two sisters on the table opposite. They stoop over their plates and pick neatly at their food in tandem. They wear around their waists two matching green batik *longhis*, bought from the local covered market. Mrs Macrae had lived in longhis for an entire year. She worked the fields in them, bathed in the village river with one wrapped round her chest. She slept under one on the hard dung floor of her mud hut. She had been so desperate to live the life of the native, and would scoff at the tourists in their air-conditioned cars, whilst she sat hot and squashed on a sack of paw-paws at the back of the local bus. And if it had been possible to change the colour of her skin then, she surely would have done.

Towards the end of the meal Mr Abdullah appears in the doorway. He claps his hands and starts to bellow orders to his houseboys. They scuttle off like beetles. He swaggers over to the Macraes with the confident air of a man who holds sway over many things.

'Everything OK?' he shouts.

'Wonderful.' Mrs Macrae makes a ball of rice and curry with her fingers, then lifts it to her mouth and flicks it deftly in with her thumb.

'Ah, I see you eat like a native.' He slaps a mosquito from his neck. Mrs Macrae smiles.

'We've arranged with your driver, Pathi, to go to Sigiriya tomorrow as you suggested,' she says.

'Ah, our wonderful ancient fortress. Lion Rock. King Kassyapa. What an old scoundrel he was. You know, he had 500 wives up in that rock palace of his.' He chuckles, his belly, fat as the village merchant, wobbling like a wattalappam pudding. 'And you must see the frescoes of the maidens. They are not to be missed.' He puts a hand on her shoulder and leans towards her. His eyes are black, hard as marbles. 'When you return, I shall arrange a little traditional Ayurvedic massage for you.' He points at some photographs on the wall of a massage clinic. 'He's very good, you know, is Matthew. I go once a week.' He squeezes the top of her shoulder. 'You should go and release some of this Scottish tension.' His laughter resounds round the room. He wanders round the other guests like a king in his court.

Mrs Macrae returns to her journal. She reads another entry. Mr Macrae cracks open another bottle of Lion beer, ice cold from the dining room fridge.

'Just like you remember?' he asks.

'I was just thinking how strange it is, how memory plays such tricks on us.' She takes a sip from her husband's beer. 'When I came home – oh, I don't know – I felt I'd left some of my heart out here. I loved this place. But reading these again,' she fingers the yellowing pages of the journal, 'I was quite unhappy, especially at first.' Her journal has reminded her of the tropical ulcers, the endless searing heat, the loneliness, the loss of everything familiar, her wish to feel the cold Edinburgh haar on her face again. Her memory has touched everything up, embellishing the good, erasing the bad. She watches the condensation dribble down the brown beer bottle, like sweat off an oily limb.

The climb is more arduous than she remembers. To her, this fifth-century fortress has always looked like an immense red-brown rump rising up from an ocean of jungle as if from nowhere. Sigiriya. The rock throbs with the sun's midday heat. Everywhere dust clouds hang above the rust-coloured earth. They have long drunk their stores of water. Above them, as they climb, two kites swirl in the thermals. A guide has appeared from nowhere to help Eilidh up the long ascent. Eilidh wants none of it.

'Yande!' Mrs Macrae shouts, somewhat abruptly, but the guide grasps Eilidh's hand even more firmly and drags her protesting upward. She knows she will have to hand him a hefty tip. The sundress she is wearing, a white halter-neck splashed with red poppies, is tight-fitting and totally impractical for climbing. And the red dust is everywhere, under her armpits, around the edge of her knickers, itching inside her bra. Her face feels gritty. Sweat blooms in grey patches through the cotton fabric. She sees the sensible attire of all the other visitors – cool polo shirts, airy shorts, stout boots – and feels a fool.

They continue their ascent. Solid iron steps manufactured and installed by the British are still riveted to the side of the rock. Wasps buzz out from the nests that collect in the overhangs. She grasps the stout metal handrail and doesn't look down. At the top, Pathi beckons them to a large flat stone, King Kassyapa's throne. They sit on it and look out over the plain below, an unfurling carpet of foaming jungle all the way to the ocean.

'Tamil Tigers hide in there – waiting to pounce.' Pathi springs like a civet towards them. They all jump. Mrs Macrae frowns at Pathi.

'Hey, they not interested in the likes of you,' he says, and his sad eyes look down at his feet. Mrs Macrae frowns at Pathi. She wishes he hadn't mentioned the war. It is not the Sri Lanka she remembers.

'I must show you the frescoes,' she says to Mr Macrae, changing the subject. There is a clamour of resistance from all three children. Mr Macrae shrugs. Pathi agrees to take the young ones back down to the jeep where he has cold drinks waiting.

'You two go,' Pathi says. 'You go make love with the Maidens.' He winks at them both.

Mr and Mrs Macrae tread carefully back down the steep staircase, and weave their way through to a walkway gouged out of the rock, shielded by a tall highly polished wall. She takes his hand, leading the way. It is hot and slippery.

'It's called the Mirror Wall. Look!' She points at swirls of ancient graffiti etched into the rock. 'Over fifteen hundred years old. They're all verses inspired by the frescoes. Erotic poems of love.'

Mr Macrae lets go of her hand and squeezes her bottom.

'And lust?' he growls.

'Not here!' She moves quickly away, avoiding his gaze.

The bejewelled damsels chalked into the rock are even more beautiful than she recalls. The colours still vibrant. The perfect breasts swelling out of the red granite. The full and sensual lips. The deep, mango-curved navels. Translucent veils as thin as butterfly wings tickling their nipples, so fragile they might flutter away in the slightest breeze.

They stand there for some minutes, lost in contemplation. Did these creatures really exist, she wonders, or are they a fantasy made perfect by their artist?

She continues to ponder this question on the drive back to Kandy in the cool of their air-conditioned jeep. They pass another army checkpoint. Since Pathi has spoken of it, she notices every one; the wooden shacks shrouded in palm fronds and piled high with oil drums and sandbags, over which white eyes peer out from the shadows, guns glinting.

The sign above the door is modest. Matthew. U. Guneratue, Ayurvedic Masseur. The black letters have been hand-painted on a rough piece of bare wood. Mrs Macrae leaves her shoes at the door and enters. Her poppy sundress is now soaked through with dust and sweat. There has been no time to freshen up. The door opens onto a small reception area with cheap plastic seats and a low wooden table. On it, stands a vase of red anthuriums. She marvels at their waxy red heart-shaped flowers and the long creamy spikes that protrude from their centres. They don't look real. Beneath her feet the asphalt floor is cool and smooth. To the back of the reception area yellow moth-eaten curtains are drawn. There is a shuffling of feet.

'Matthew?' calls Mrs Macrae, and a man emerges from behind the curtain drying his hands. She had expected a wiry individual clad in sarong, not this huge bulk of a man in pink shorts, flip-flops and stripy shirt.

'Sorry for delay.' Matthew smiles, his clean white teeth gleam like strip-lights next to his dark skin.

'Mr Abdullah rang on my behalf. Grace Macrae.' She extends her hand to his. His grip is strong and her hand feels crushed. He beckons her to sit down on one of the red plastic chairs. She knows her thighs will stick to them in this heat, and will peel off like Elastoplasts, so she perches herself on the edge.

'Here – read some of these while I get ready.' He hands her an old blue jotter, just like the ones she used to have in primary school, with ruled feint, red margin and rough scratchy paper. She reads:

Man! There are massages and massages, and jeezo, does Matthew do the latter.

Matthew's fingers are the strongest I've encountered. A deep tissue massage of the first order.

I'd recommend Matthew's massages to anyone. His kind demeanour and sensitive touch makes this an out-of-body experience.

Every entry glowed.

'You read them?' He asks, smiling, as he returns with a clay pot in his hands.

'Hari hundai.' Very good.

'So, you speak Singhalese?'

'Okome mateke ne.' Forgotten all of it. He laughs.

'Come'. He ushers her into a changing cubicle in the corner. 'Just take your clothes off and wrap up in this towel.'

A rusty nail is the only thing Mrs Macrae can find on which to hang her discarded clothes. A full-length mirror leans against the wall in front of her. It is cracked through at head height and is clouded with dirt. Her body is streaked with Sigiriya dust and her shoulders and neck are an angry red. If somebody gave her husband a piece of chalk and a granite wall, is that how he would draw her? Just as she is. Or would he modify the camembert stomach, the low-slung breasts; erase the mole on her shoulder, give her a waist again, smooth out the lines on her face? Would he depict truth or fantasy? She picks up a towel and hurriedly wraps it round her. It is damp and grubby, and is stained with oil. She pulls back the curtain. Matthew has placed a wooden chair for her just outside. She sits down in front of the cracked mirror. He stands behind her and begins to massage her head and shoulders with some of the oil from his clay pot. Her burnt face shines like a grilled prawn.

'If you prefer, you can lie, but I prefer this. Better contact.' He thrusts his hips forward, burying his fingers in her dust-caked scalp. He is good. She loses herself to the sensations, watching him in the mirror. He tells her he has just returned from Good Friday Mass. Mrs Macrae has clean forgotten. Not a chocolate egg in sight to remind her. Of course, with a name like Matthew, he has to be a Christian. He talks of his eight brothers and sisters with whom he still lives in a small village a few miles from Kandy. She tells him of Scotland, of her family, of the ceaseless rain they have left behind. They fill the room with harmless chatter and laughter. He continues to knead her shoulders, head and neck, his fingers firm and sure.

'Grease! You're so tense – come back tomorrow and I do it free of charge. Okay?'

Grease. Mrs Macrae laughs inwardly at the pronunciation of her name. She feels exactly like that. A filthy greaseball. Matthew towers above her, still working on the muscles at the top of her neck. The crack in the mirror makes him appear beheaded. She watches his flexing biceps. He tells her of his seven years training.

'You have to be strong. Very strong.' Matthew shows her his fists, clenches and unclenches them. Pink. Brown. Pink. Brown. So pale his palms, she thinks. So white his teeth. And almost as an afterthought, how kind his eyes. She feels her body begin to float. She asks him what Ayurvedic means.

'Ayu, this mean *"life"*. Veda, this mean *"knowledge"*. Life knowledge. It's very ancient, Grease. A medicine that's been around for thousand of years.'

Life knowledge. She likes that. The oils are absorbing into her hot skin. Sesame oil, a waft of sandalwood perhaps, and the smell of rusting metal. Matthew does not know the English words.

'Special, rare oils with herbs. All sorts,' he shrugs, guiding her up from the chair over to a slatted wooden bench. Fragrant oils in clay bowls line one end. Mrs Macrae clambers onto the high bench, trying not to lose her towel, which she has to unfasten and throw over her back. She is aware of Matthew watching her. It would have been easier to throw the towel off and slide on elegantly, but it's too late now. It has become bunched under her stomach and Matthew has to wrench it out from under her and rearrange it over her back so that only her legs are visible. He closes the moth-eaten curtains and begins with her feet.

'Hikkaduwa, you go Hikkaduwa?'

'No,' Mrs Macrae says, 'not that hippy dump. I've heard it's ruined now.'

'Sad place, Grease. Very sad. Lots of drugs and bad people. Men paying for small boys. This place Hikkaduwa is where I first practise.'

Mrs Macrae tries to imagine this big gentle giant on the white sand amongst the ponytails and clouds of hashish smoke. It seems incongruous. He pummels her bunched calves. She flinches.

'I hurt? Sorry, Grease. I will be gentler with you. My hands too strong sometimes.' He begins to work on her back. Mrs Macrae feels herself falling into a slumber of sorts, a soporific haze of contentment. Outside she hears the grumble of rush-hour traffic on the Sangaraja Mawatha, the persistent horns of the tuk-tuks as they weave in and out, the shrill signature tune of the Walls Ice Cream vendor. She is utterly relaxed.

Then quite without warning he removes her towel and flips her over onto her back. His head looms close. His breath is hot on her cheek.

'Grease. Is it okay to do here?' His voice is almost a whisper. He points at her stomach.

'Yes, of course,' she says, grateful that he should ask.

'And here?' He points at her breasts. Mrs Macrae hesitates. She is unsure of how to respond, but Mr Abdullah's words *traditional* and *Ayurvedic* ring loud in her ears. She thinks it would be priggish to refuse.

'And down here, too?' He points vaguely in the direction of her lower abdomen.

'Sure.'

He begins to smooth her belly with both hands.

'Terrible, these stretch marks,' she says, and she tries a nonchalant laugh, but it comes out all strangled.

But Matthew says nothing, spiralling inwards over her navel with his fingertips, like two cobras coiling down to sleep. His palms lie hot and unmoving for several moments, then, as if the snakes are slowly stretching awake, they slide upwards over her oiled belly and gently cup her breasts. She does not breathe. There is no sound in the room save his soft breath feathering in the hot air above her.

'People say Matthew have magic fingers.' His voice is slow and thick. Nothing moves. She looks up. His dark eyes stare down at her. And then it comes, and she knows it's coming and it's too late to stop it, this blush of skin-pricking heat that rises to the surface of her skin from the tips of her feet to her scalp. She closes her eyes. Her pulse is thumping. She lies immobile, waiting.

And, briefly, as she lies there under the heat of his palms, a memory looms. She's at the top of the slide, the really big, shiny steel slide in Inverleith Park, the one that reaches halfway to the sky, the one she's always wanted to go on, and now that she's five years old she can, and she's sitting up there at the top for the first time, up high like a bird in a tree, but she can't go down. It is a cold winter afternoon. She is shivering. The pom-pom on her knitted woollen hat is buffeted by the stiff easterly wind. Her red Start-Rite shoes kick the steel making a booming sound. Her legs are bruised with cold. She grasps the green metal rail with its blistering paint. Her knuckles are white. Her nose is running. Her mother stands with outstretched arms at the bottom, calling encouraging words, but Grace can't hear her, and there's queues of other kids bunching up behind her, all taunting 'Come on ye fearty – scaredy custard!' and her stomach is in her mouth and she can't look down at that vast river of steel, polished by thousands of others. She just grips the rails with her tiny pink hands and cannot let go.

And Mrs Macrae cannot move as Matthew slowly encircles her breasts, then her nipples. And she chooses to interpret the first brush of his hands between her legs as an accident. It is only when he parts her legs a little further and a finger slithers inside her that she knows what is about to happen. She is aware only of the tremor of his breath, and a fat brown slug of a finger inside her. Flesh on flesh, flesh in flesh. And a wet sound like a child sucking on a gobstopper. And all the while the fingers of his other hand encircle her nipples, first one, then the other, slowly, slowly and then with increasing speed. And Mrs Macrae is five years old again. On top of the slide and terrified.

Jesus, think of something. Should she jump up, slap his face? Tell him where to shove his goddamned fingers. She plays out a series of scenes in her mind, scenes of outrage and indignation. But she knows she cannot do it to him. And she knows the reason why: she is too scared to *offend* the man.

And she begins to think that if she can't offend him, then perhaps she should play the part that Matthew wishes. Yield to his touch. She could tilt her hips, arch her back, and move to his rhythm. She could part her lips and moan. She could let go of the rusting handrail, and slip down the mirror of steel, and feel the wind on her face and the exhilaration and the speed. She could throw her head back, watch the gulls and the clouds sail past. She could roar like a lion, wild and free. But what if she does yield? Would Matthew then clamber on top of her, thrust in deep, and continue where his finger left off?

And, for a moment, she is back on the silver slide again, but it is not her mother who stands there at the bottom waiting for her. It is Matthew, smiling, his arms outstretched, his hands clasping and unclasping, pink brown, pink brown like giant Venus flycatchers. She stands up, naked, holding her Sigiriya sundress, her stretch marks flame-red against her white belly. And she stinks of the inside of her and the acrid oils, which spill out of her pores and burn her flesh. Mrs Macrae tries to descend. She teeters on the top step, but loses her footing and falls. She falls down her slide that's halfway to the sky, tumbling towards Matthew and the kind eyes and the white teeth and the monstrous hands. And she prays she will keep on falling, falling, because then it will all be a dream, in which the bottom will never be reached.

'Enough, Matthew. I think enough.' Her words are fractured, barely audible, her mouth dry, her tongue thick. She feels a nausea rising in the back of her throat. He stops immediately, removing his finger as though a fish has bitten it. She opens her eyes. He paces the room for a few moments, like a trapped tiger, then is beside her again, his face close to hers. It is wet with perspiration and his eyes are afraid. He speaks between clenched teeth.

'Grease, Grease. I asked you and you say *yes*. Okay? You say *yes*.'

'I didn't think you meant where you did.' It sounds feeble, unconvincing. He grabs a cloth from behind her head and dries his hands. He does not speak for some moments. When he does, there is the slightest hint of menace to his tone.

'You want me to say to your husband what we did together? What do you think he would say, I wonder?'

We did. His words hit her like a thrust stone. But she must look appalled, as he sits down quickly beside her and takes her hand.

'Of course, Grease, I won't tell. What goes on behind this curtain is a secret, okay?' His hand trembles. 'Listen, I just poor village boy doing job for my boss.'

Mrs Macrae thinks of a man on a hillside not far from here with marble eyes and a belly that wobbles. And there is one last question that she knows she must ask, that hangs in the hot air like a lifeboat from a sinking vessel.

'Was that, you know, what you did, was that *traditional*

Ayurvedic massage?' It will be all right, she thinks, if she can put this thing into the realms of something ancient and oriental.

Matthew looks at her in horror, as though she has desecrated a holy shrine. 'Not that last thing. Oh no! Not *that*.'

Later, back home, Mrs Macrae will tell her story many times over many dinners. Her words will silence the clink of crystal and clatter of silver on bone china, and she will revel in the telling, in the drama of the moment: the shifting discomfort of the men, the squawks of disbelief from the women. And the tight laughter when it comes will burst forth from their throats like escaping champagne and cause their ribs to ache. This will be her comedy act, her public version.

Privately, though, as Mr Macrae lies beside her on the cusp of sleep, she will call out softly into the dark, 'Langete ende mathe.' Come closer. And she will begin to scratch another kind of curling script into the Mirror Wall of her memory: verses inspired by the perfect fresco of a black man with kind eyes and magic touch, an image that she will chalk and chalk with bare hands into the rough red granite, until her knuckles bleed.

MIKE GREENHOUGH
Mercury Rising

Guy's little key turned easily in the plywood door. The mailbox was generously proportioned, with a volume and aperture suited to a far more popular person. It was just one of an eight-by-eight array of similar units, newly installed and, as yet, sparsely populated. A slot on the front carried a slip of paper with his name; the untidy, pencilled capitals reflected his tenancy – recent, hasty, tentative. He rifled unhopefully through the contents. No party invitations, sonnets, billets-doux or Milk Tray from secret admirers. Not even a final demand. Just a slim pile of junk mail.

The large, draughty entrance hall of Marlborough Mansions was littered with trestles, sawdust and timber offcuts – flotsam from a noisy and erratic programme of refurbishment, creeping through the vast Victorian building, drawing in a trickle of new residents in its wake. Guy crossed the hall to his flatlet, one of the first to be finished. Being on the ground floor it was slightly grander, or at least less *bijou*, than many others. It was also somewhat stark and lacking in character, though the builders, either by negligence or design, had left in place some original features – plaster mouldings, a ceiling rose, an ancient fireplace. The paint was dry to the touch but still fresh enough to irritate lung and nostril. He opened the window on to a tiny bare courtyard. Birdsong and distant traffic drifted in, mingling with the whine of power drills and sanders.

Seating himself in the armchair Guy unfolded a leaflet from the top of the mail pile. *Staytite Glazing* were making *UNRE-PEATABLE OFFERS*. And, what was more, their team of highly trained representatives was at the moment operating in that very area, dispensing free, no-obligation quotes. The next item was a glossy, midnight-blue envelope festooned with zodiacal symbols. He slit it open. 'Griselda', from *Cosmic Concerns*, was offering guidance to the astrally perplexed. A third communication, marked *GRAND INTERNATIONAL PRIZE-DRAW GIVEAWAY*, he declined to open altogether. One can take only so much philanthropy at a time.

The evening air already held some hints of autumn, but of a kind more chill than mellow. Guy pulled on an old knitted cardigan. A thousand wearings had only served to increase its lopsidedness, along with his own fondness for it. A gift from her to him, Christmases ago, it still felt and smelled right – love and incompetence, timelessly interwoven. He fastened the buttons and picked up the mail again. Unrepeatable offers, indeed. Communication seemed to have reached a low ebb. Just as she had so recently claimed. He scrunched the papers into a single ball and tossed it into the empty firegrate. Now connections had been severed. Had to be, she'd declared; they both needed some space and time. It was an unanswer-able assertion – one qualified just by being alive and three-dimensional. Guy put a match to the paper, prompting a short, merry blaze – a brief candle of comfort in the gathering dusk.

Over the next week promoters of dubious goods and services stepped up the postal bombardment of the new occupants of Marlborough Mansions. There was evidently something in the address that suggested just the right mix of credulity and disposable income. Each day Guy viewed his own crop of mail with resignation, skimming the odd, legitimate item from the mounting pile of unsolicited dross. On Saturday, with darkness fallen and curtains closed, he drew the armchair up to the fireplace and cast a final eye over the now substantial bundle. It made uniformly unpersuasive reading.

> *Fame and Riches can be yours!*
> *An Edwardian conservatory with a difference!*
> *Two unique magnetic bracelets for the price of one!*

And so on, and on.

He responded to the string of exhortations and promises with a single match. Catalogues of optimism, hyperbole and plain old deceit blistered and blazed, gladdening the heart, bringing comfort to fingers and toes. The curling smoke was drawn up through a maze of ancient flues and drifted unseen from high forgotten chimney pots. The few moments of cheeriness left an afterglow which somehow lingered till he was ready for bed. And as he brushed his teeth he could have sworn the tap water was just a little less cold than before.

Passing the array of mailboxes on his daily exits and entrances Guy watched with interest the slow sprouting of name labels as newcomers staked their claims. Their choice of position seemed governed by a curious haphazardness. In general they shunned the exposed border regions – perhaps out of some self-protective, herd instinct – but avoided direct chumminess; settling close to, but not contiguous with, already occupied sites. Were they just opting for a row and column convenient to their own height and hardness? Or taking a consciously whimsical approach – indulging in a little anarchy to offset the indignity of being pigeon-holed at all? Bucking the general trend Guy had taken the top right corner box, thus commanding two sides and a diagonal. A certain Ms Goodwin, on the other hand, announcing herself in bold green biro, had chosen top left – a sound tactical response, perhaps, in some giant, residents' noughts-and-crosses challenge.

It was the same Ms G. who one morning chanced upon Guy, dressing-gowned and unshaven, frowning over his mail in the dimly lit hallway.

'Bad news?' she ventured.

'I've been specially chosen,' said Guy absently, waving a letter plastered with lurid, legal-looking scrollwork and gigantic golden pound signs.

'Congratulations!' She slipped away up the stairs before he could properly register the congenial smile and ironic lift of eyebrow, or, indeed, the silky black hair peeping out from under a fluffy white towel.

With little furniture, no television and no contact from the old address, the space and time Guy had been assured he needed was now available in abundance. Though nine-to-five was accounted for by office routine, and extended either end by a short walk and a long bus-ride, a lot of hours remained unfilled.

Mail poured in, bringing offers of ever greater scope and

unmissability – offers of alleviation and of betterment, financial, spiritual and corporeal: saunas and solaria, auras and gurus, tattoos and timeshare. By October, dealing with the week's waste had become a regular Saturday-night fixture. There were countless items, but few worth agonising over.

Double your income!
Realign your spiritual energies!
Develop an irresistible personality!

The process of disposal took on a ritual, repetitive format – inquisition, denouncement, gleeful commitment to the flames. But then a single lapse of vigilance brought a near miscarriage of justice, when a slim, bona fide gas bill, sandwiched between bulky offers on stone cladding and reincarnation, narrowly escaped the fire. Perhaps it was indeed time to develop a new personality.

To the sender of each subsequent unsolicited offer Guy returned a slip of paper stating that the previous occupant had died, and signed *Mr Phoenix*. He had a copy made of his little key and filed away at the crudely shaped wards till it fitted the empty mailbox below his own. This he duly assigned to Mr P., who within days was receiving more mail than his begetter ever had. Senders were clearly overwhelmed that somebody out there had actually, voluntarily, written *to* *them*. For promoters of orthopaedic beds, crystal balls or fitted kitchens, this was as close as you got to being loved.

Remove unsightly blemishes!
Transform your life!
Amaze your friends!

First one had to acquire them. Climbing the Mansion steps one evening Guy looked up to see Ms Goodwin striding down. She eyed the bag of bananas, newspaper and pint of milk he was embracing.

'Slimming?'

'Well. No. Just popped out for a few, odd things.' He rearranged the articles in his grasp, to no particular effect. There would have been a silence but for light traffic and a mob of local sparrows. Even allowing for the two-step height advantage, she was tallish, willowy, self-possessed: a woman who would change her own light bulbs.

'Well, better get along,' said Guy vaguely, and continued the climb.

Harness your biorhythms!
Astral projection in under a week!

Burning was simply too good for some items; anything above and beyond the level of routine irksomeness and fraudulence, Guy took to returning in the envelope provided – always unstamped and often with brusque annotations in red biro. Far from having a discouraging effect this seemed only to increase the number and inanity of communications, as senders redoubled their own efforts and sold the name on to cognate companies. A live respondent like Mr Phoenix was clearly to be treasured and cultivated. In time, they must have reasoned, with the patience of seasoned psychotherapists, he might be coaxed into including the required payment. Or at least filling in the application form. Or at the very least refraining from sending it back in shreds.

Soon Guy's own mailbox was back to receiving a more modest and largely sensible load. That of Mr Phoenix, however, was regularly brimful. And so it was that a *Mr Ash* was spawned and moved into the next box below. Guy, posing as Mr P., then introduced Mr A. to a particularly dogged distributor of encyclopaedias, thus procuring for the two of them, respectively, an allegedly *Stylish Ball-point Pen* and a *Handsome Leatherette Wallet*. These bonus items, being judged tawdry but of low calorific value, were set aside as potential stocking fillers. The commercial grapevine duly sprang into action, showering the newest member of the community with voluminous and combustible offers and advice. Next Saturday night Guy enjoyed a long, leisurely burn-up courtesy of Messrs P. and A., subsequently turning down the radiator a couple of notches and noting triumphantly an unmistakable rise in the tap-water temperature. Evidently the old back boiler was still connected and functional.

But triumph was tinged with a creeping unease. Did one ever really get something for nothing? Surely there were always hidden costs and constraints. From the inviolable laws of thermodynamics to a local borough council's clean-air legislation, all acts of energy conversion were subject to regulation and penalty. That night his dreams were filled with the sighs of distant rain forests, tainted by the confused and troubling chemistries of ozone, smog and acid rain. He awoke late, and tired, but anxious to begin redressing the imbalances.

The bulk of Sunday he devoted to three redeeming, mile-long trudges to the garden centre, each time returning heavily laden. By evening the tiny concrete courtyard was graced by a huge wooden half-barrel, three-quarters full of mulch and crowned with a lank but promising little magnolia tree.

Open at once! This is NOT a circular . . .
Failure to respond constitutes forfeiture of your assigned
  entitlement.
Banish baldness!
You have been specially chosen!

The format was familiar but the pound signs had got even bigger.

The messages got more resistible by the day. There was no need even to read the things. Different kinds of nonsense burn equally well. The message was irrelevant, the medium was all. Guy began to look forward to each day's delivery, rising early to gather his new-found source of fuel.

But not always early enough.

'Good morning.'

Guy started at the voice. It was soft, but sudden – Ms Goodwin's approach having been muted by luxurious and pomponed carpet slippers.

'*Some*body's popular today!' She eyed the bulky assortment of envelopes.

'Oh, it's mostly junk. I expect, anyway.' He clutched the bundle closer to his chest.

'Not your birthday then?'

'No. Not till April.'

'Really?' Her gaze returned to his face. 'I had you down as a fellow Scorpio.'

Guy brightened. 'You mean, like, spontaneous and inventive?'

'That's Gemini, isn't it?'

'Could be, I just made it up.'

'So did I, actually.' She stroked her still-damp hair. Even in the dimness it had lustre, luxuriance, an undeniable strokeability.

There was a surprisingly unawkward ten-second pause. Then they both said 'Well', simultaneously, exchanged conventional nodding smiles, and departed to their respective breakfasts.

Week by week the stream of advertising grew. With November began some distinctly seasonal tendencies. A glut of offers on double glazing and cavity-wall insulation gave way to a flurry of storm porches, and then a positive epidemic of thermal socks and vests. These added their considerable weight to the regular daily dose of overseas lotteries and divination, psychic messengers and visionaries, numerology and planet power.

To keep up with the influx Guy constantly expanded the accommodation, and by the start of Advent his little community occupied a whole vertical column of mailboxes. It was quite unnecessary to open everything that arrived, but random samples, taken for routine monitoring purposes, enlivened his coffee and toast on many a chill grey morning:

> *My Dear Mrs Burnham,*
> *The cards tell me that people often take you for granted. In fact there are times when they behave as if you didn't exist at all . . .*
> *Frankly, Mr Fahrenheit, we don't offer a Super Platinum Plus Star Trust Account card to just anyone . . .*

See our exciting range of invisible hearing aids!
Read these unbelievable testimonials!
Unleash that inner calm!

The fuel supply was now sufficient for a cheery blaze most evenings, with the bonus of a shave in the morning and a small but significant reduction in gas consumption. But harvesting and processing the paper crop demanded a good deal of caution. Guy was only too aware that adopting multiple aliases, and receiving and disposing of a prodigious post might invite a variety of misconstructions. Often he would wait till after dark, when things were quiet and the hallway's dim lighting offered some cover. With further, careful filing his little key had acquired a skeletal, master status, though it sometimes needed a protracted wiggling to work its effect. While thus engaged – eyes squinting, protruding tongue echoing the intricate, probing twists – there was little chance of his detecting Ms Goodwin's approach across the newly laid carpet.

'Checking on the neighbours?' She raised a single eyebrow a good inch or so.

Guy forced himself to remain calm. 'Oh. He's abroad, actually. I'm, sort of, looking after things. In effect.'

She stared pointedly at an envelope he held between his ankles. It was much larger, plainer and browner than he might have wished. 'That's very charitable of you.'

He shrugged. 'Well, what are neighbours for. After all?'

'Is he gone for long?'

Guy swallowed. 'Hard to say, really. He's a bit of a mystery man. Between you and me, that is.'

'You must introduce me some time.' She gave him the full

eyebrow treatment, both barrels, followed by a conciliatory smile. Her hair was up, as if for a formal function, though the jeans and t-shirt suggested something more domestic.

It was clear that the collection of mail had to be speeded up and somehow simplified. Loitering and going equipped, even in one's own building, were decidedly bad for the image. Late that night, with just a screwdriver and pliers, Guy effected a clandestine merger of the various parties in his column of conspirators by prising up and removing the plywood floorlets which separated the compartments. This ensured that subsequent deliveries to any one of them would now, through gravity alone, end up c/o *Mr Poole*, the occupant of the lowest box.

The days grew colder. The nights, colder still. His letters to the old address were unanswered. Were they sitting on the sideboard unopened or unread? Were they perhaps suffering a fiery fate of their own? It looked increasingly as if the time and space he'd been given were to become permanent.

And so he began to spend some of the time in filling the space. Pre-Christmas, office-lunch-hour shopping sprees yielded a succession of items to enhance the cosiness of hearth and home – a shiny brass companion set, a commodious coal scuttle, a large and luxurious fireside rug. He bought handtools too, for the fitting of fixtures (or was it the fixing of fittings?) and for any more ambitious projects which might come along. It all began to feel a little less unlike home.

Dear Occupier,
As one of our most loyal and valued customers you have been

awarded a luxury cruise, a limousine, a villa in Spain, or
an exquisite and valuable pendant!
Channel the heavenly influences!
Become unimaginably rich! (postmarked Croydon)
You have been specially chosen!

What did one have to do to be specially ignored?

Sunday mornings he tended the little tree, keeping it watered, packing a bucketful of yesterday's fine grey ashes around the roots, fancying that it perked up visibly after each trodden instalment, as it absorbed the dense, nutritious compost of defunct deviousness and quackery. More than once he sensed a curtain twitch in the window above his own. Was there an observer up there with time and interest enough to piece together his various stratagems? Or would he be dismissed as merely eccentric? Either way, if fuel levels increased any further he might have to consider alternative disposal techniques. It said 'NO ASHES' on the council bin bags, and flushing the stuff might bring appalling long-term consequences. Perhaps one could take a tip from those irrepressible tunnellers in POW-camp films – take a jaunty stroll around the neighbourhood, opportunely slackening hidden drawstrings to release the incriminating material from the ends of trouser legs.

Then again, it's possible to be over-discreet. The first rule of counter-intelligence is to not let them know that you know. But it's tricky if you don't know exactly *whom* to not let know. And in the anonymous vastness of the Mansions it was very hard to know who was who, and where. The population was still on the increase – constant sound, carried through the structure, told of widespread activity, but not of its location. Faint intermittent thudding by day suggested the builders were now nearing the far end of the block. Lighter-duty, more domestic tapping and drilling went on late into the evening, as, here and there, nameless and numberless appliances were plumbed, fittings fitted and fixtures fixed, keeping the building resonating with nebulous human endeavour, like some benign, peacetime Colditz Castle.

Occasionally, more local, though no less intriguing, sounds came through the ceiling – a faint clatter of heels, the rhythmic thump of a sewing (or *rowing*?) machine, short bouts of coughing (Saturday nights especially) and once in a while the tentative staccato of a manual typewriter. Perhaps one should take the initiative – tap on the door with a late-night request for fuse wire or a cup of sugar. But in the still-unnumbered flats and bedsits on just which door would one tap?

One could be surer, more intriguing, even a little cryptic, with a mailbox message. Guy sifted through the pile of recent unsought wisdom received, snipping out fragments of advice, celestial and mundane, and pasted them on to a blank sheet. A little verse, unavoidably irregular in font and meter, took shape before his eyes:

Scorpio: *Take care, your curiosity may get the better*
of you
I enclose an UNREPEATABLE offer
time to make new friends *and keep warm*
this winter

Guy wasn't entirely sure what it meant, but it did have a

pleasing kind of gnomic, haiku feel, with perhaps just a hint of the ransom note. He posted it in the top left mailbox. The green-biroed name had been replaced by elite typeface, slightly smudged, and had acquired initials. Somebody was planning to be here for a while.

As the influx of mail increased so it plumbed ever greater depths of mindlessness. Guy would put aside the most extreme examples, behind the clock, until a small collection of uniform stupidity had accumulated. The contents were then thoroughly shuffled before being returned in random envelopes. He was half hoping to confuse and annoy his newly found enemies, even foster a few internecine conflicts. But this criss-crossing just seemed to breed an ever greater and more resilient supply of nonsense. From time to time transcription errors produced mutant but viable variations of the recipients' surnames, leading to further proliferation. Local leafleteers paid daily visits to the Mansions, heavily laden with adverts for craft fairs and home improvement. Grateful for the privacy of the hallway, they disgorged multiple copies into each of the accommodating slots, which yawned irresistibly like row upon regular row of insatiable nestlings.

Dear Major Burns,
I feel I have known you a long time, and I sense confusion in your life . . .

Dear Mrs Bunsen,
You have omitted to sign your membership activation form . . .

You are going to meet a tall, dark stranger. (This on an otherwise blank postcard)

What do you desire? Love, Luck, Fame, Fortune?

Tick the box; sign the form.

Write the cheque.

There was no end to it: elixirs and immortality, oracles and miracles, stair lifts and loft conversions. For Guy, sceptical, able-bodied and loftless, there could be only one reaction to such material. And it was simple, swift and satisfyingly exothermic.

As his own column in the mailbox array came close to capacity he established a couple of outposts – small foreign enclaves occupied, respectively, by a 'Mr Hibachi' and a 'Herr Kindling' – not altogether implausible recipients, given the cosmopolitan neighbourhood of the Mansions. But the take-over of the surrounding boxes by more legitimate settlers put a limit on his imperial ambitions. Where to go from here? Soaking in a long, hot bath – his first achieved entirely from alternative energy – Guy had a *Eureka*! moment.

When all was quiet he began to make little sorties into the furthest reaches of the building, picking up sizeable scraps of plywood and two-by-two which had been cluttering the corridors (a man could have tripped!) Occasionally, he fancied shadows and footsteps behind, though there was nothing in the dimness when he turned. Back in the flatlet, with the rug rolled up and the curtains closed, he set to work.

Days passed. There was no response to the 'poem', unless it had somehow got itself lost among the reams of paper. Of the occupant of the flat above there was no sight, and little sound. Perhaps the late-night sawing, multiple personalities and singular furtiveness had finally proved unnerving.

Dear Rear Admiral Towcester,
I can help you get in touch with your true self . . .
Enlist the vibrations of the cosmos!
Channel your energy flows!

Pyramids and patios, mystics and mediums, shamans and shams.

By early December the carpentry was complete. Guy poured himself a glass of wine and sat watching with some pride as the last coat of varnish dried. In the ensuing small hours he was able to install his master work – a full-size, passable imitation of the mailboxes – on the outside wall of his own flatlet, opposite the established array. It sported eight-by-eight plausible-looking, if unopenable, doors, complete with dummy keyholes, and real, generous apertures. Inside, it was empty except for a long, polished plank running the length of the base, and propped up at one end to form a gentle slope. This funnelled all incoming mail into the one openable 'box' in the bottom left corner – the domicile of one 'Mr Hopper'.

Using a combination of his previous escalation strategies Guy soon had the name slots filled and the whole unit receiving unprecedented amounts of what was surely a fuel of the future – sealed in dense, weighty, white or manila envelopes; free, clean, easy to handle, and packed with British Thermal Units. Christmas was coming. He bought in nuts, mince pies and Bristol Cream, ensuring comfort, if not joy, for the holiday.

On the morning of Christmas Eve Guy awoke to find the magnolia tree topped by a shining silver fairy. Over breakfast he watched in wonder as it twinkled in the pale sunshine. Then the mail van arrived. To unload the new box took him a number of trips. Too big a number. It was time for the final breakthrough. A matter of minutes with a masonry drill and the back entrance to Mr Hopper's domain became accessible from inside the flatlet. Below the hole he placed the roomy brass coal scuttle, to receive incoming material. Just above it he installed a little hook – in the event of visitors this allowed the hole to be quickly covered by a large, framed print depicting the Last Judgement.

Evening came, snow was forecast, but seemed unlikely. In the stillness of Marlborough Mansions, with firelight flickering across his face, Guy poured himself a large sherry and drank to absent friends, and self-sufficiency. Just a few feet behind him, courtesy of the indefatigable deliverers of pamphlets and catalogues, winter fuel was still gathering itself. From the armchair, he gazed into the flames – the purifying, all-consuming flames – dancing in time and space, powering the great cycle of life. Ashes to ashes. Acorns to oaks. He glanced around the room – his room. Time and space. What more could a man want? Apart from luck and love, fame and fortune. He closed his eyes and made a wish.

There was a tapping at the door. Guy sat a moment, waiting for an outbreak of 'Silent Night' or 'Wenceslas', but there came only further, louder tapping. He opened the door a few inches, and then widely. She had on a long dress, seasonally white, and in her glossy black hair sat a faded tinsel star.

'Mr Dante?' she grinned.

'Well, not exactly.'

'Mr Prometheus, then?'

'No, you see . . . they're all sort of, professional, pseud-onyms, or is it noms de pl . . . It's a bit hard to . . .'

She cut him short with a wand-like wave of a shiny silver toasting fork. Coupled with the tarnished tinsel it tempered her angelic air with an alluring hint of Lucifer.

'*You*, then,' she prodded him gently in the stomach with the blunt end.

'What *about* me?'

She slipped past into the room, pressing into his hands a packet of *Tiny Tim's Christmas Crumpets*. '*You,*' she whispered, 'have been specially chosen.' And this time he really had.

ANN JOLLY
Black Threads

'It won't hurt,' my father says, his voice cold and crackling like snakeskin.

'It will hurt a little,' my Mama says as she turns her face away.

My older sister says nothing. Silence has a power of its own.

On the ground in front of me are blobs of steaming elephant dung. They are the size of squared-off melons and give off the light sweet smell of well-rotted leaves. In front of me, half hidden by acacia bushes, is a line of the rolling grey backs of elephants, as familiar as the curve of my own hip. In the distance, women working in the fields of tea and maize look like specks of mosquitoes clinging to the hills. The heat of the air is on me like the hot breath of a dog and I am going to stay here on this rock in the shade of the thorn scrub until Mama calls me.

'Rozina,' I will hear her shout, 'Rozina, where are you?' Only then I will take the path back to our shamba with my water bucket balanced on my head.

I decide that until I hear her voice, I will sit beside the river watching the sun inch round the sky and safari ants stream across the earth. I poke at them with a stick and they scatter wildly, scurrying back and forth until they pick up the trail again and march on, like soldiers to war.

The village is humming with activity. The noise is like angry wasps. I'm not sure I want to think about this, so instead I think about the new dress Mama is stitching for me. The red material is patterned with yellow fish swimming through black threads of water and Mama bought it from a duka in the market. Then she shows me how to mark out the shape of the bodice on the cloth with charcoal.

'Don't make the neckline too low,' she hisses as I scissor along the lines, 'or the sixth form boys will think you are easy'.

My sister sniggers at this and I kick at her with my bare foot.

'Rozina,' I hear my Mama's voice, 'Rozina, where are you?' The sound of her comes louder and nearer so I wind the strip of old cloth into a pad and put it on my head to balance the bucket. Mama scolds me when I get back to our house.

'Where have you been?' she shouts, 'can't you see there is work to be done?'

From his chair in the shadow of the overhanging roof my father says, 'You're nearly a woman now, don't hang about down by the river or people will say you are loose. Help your mother', and he tamps tobacco into his pipe.

Mama is getting ready for tomorrow. She rolls ground nuts and pumpkin flowers into a thick brown paste, picks over rice to take out the stones and pounds maize into flour. Throughout the village, other mamas are doing the same. I catch the goat and milk her, her coarse grey hair against my cheek and her milky goat smell is familiar and comforting. Then I scour the aluminium sufuria with ash so that I can see my face when I look into it. My sister has plaited extensions into my hair and pinned them in loops so that my head looks as if it's exploding but it took her a whole afternoon to do and there is no time to change it now. I study this different version of me in the shiny bottom of the pot until Mama thrusts a broom into my hand.

'Sweep the yard,' she snaps.

Darkness is still draining from the early morning sky as I wait with my friend Esta and the other girls at the edge of the village. We are waiting for the bus to arrive. On our heads we carry folded blankets because we're going to be away from the village for several days. Our mamas are clustered importantly under a mango tree, voices a low buzz like flies on dead meat. I wear the dress Mama finished last night. Grey clouds that look like fat men's bellies gather in the distance. I drape the blanket over my shoulders because it's cold before the sun rises above the hills. When it comes up it looks like a big yellow egg yolk.

The dala dala has been specially chartered – and paid for in advance. The mamas asked for a woman driver, but the bus company doesn't have any. So they sent the ugliest man they could find.

'His face is like a baboon's bottom,' whispers Esta and I giggle because her words are tickling my ear. The driver looks frightened of us women and girls chattering and laughing as we pile into his bus.

After two hours of jolting and bumping the dala dala can

go no further. The dirt road has turned into a winding track and we have to walk. The mamas arrange for the bus to come back to collect us in four days. Four days. That's how long it will take. Our mamas chatter; of the pleasure of being away from husbands and families, of duties and digging, of the importance of this celebration and of the food they are going to cook. On their heads they carry sacks of rice, cooking pots, a live chicken or two and vegetables wrapped in newspaper. Dry season dust the colour of old nails puffs out around our feet as Esta and I swing the blue bucket filled with cups and plates between us. Butterflies dance in my belly as I think about what is to come.

'Don't break those plates,' my mama warns us.

A memory nudges me of my sister, when I asked her what would happen at this special time. Blankness spread over her face and her eyes turned hard and glassy like splinters from a broken beer bottle.

'You'll find out,' she said. Her voice was hard and glassy too.

By the time we arrive my legs are aching from the long walk and Esta has a thorn in her big toe. Our mamas sweep the space between the trees and clouds of red dust whirl all around us. We're sent off to gather wood and collect big stones to make a fireplace. Without being told, we know we must keep away from the wooden hut at the edge of the trees.

It takes the rest of the day to light the fire, prepare and cook the food. Mama hacks the chickens to death with a panga. Esta and I pluck them and the feathers stick to our hands and legs and catch in our hair so that we look like big, strange, lightly feathered birds. At last, when the sun is setting behind mottled clouds that hang in the air like rainy season fungus, the food is ready. There is rice with onions, and saffron to roll into little balls and dip in the spicy chicken, spinach with peppers, stewed fish, fried plantains and a big bowl of maize porridge. We sit in a circle and eat. Esta and I eat and eat. I have never seen so much food before at one time and I don't finish eating until a piece of the moon like an old nail paring appears in the sky. Then an ancient woman with skin as wrinkled as tree bark sings of the duties of being a woman. We join in, standing up to stamp our feet and make the noise in the back of our throats that we always do on fancy occasions like weddings or a funeral. A final thing happens. All the girls are given a drink brewed with special herbs. It tastes like nothing I've ever drunk before, sweet and sour at the same time and instead of talking as we lie rolled in our blankets under a sky splattered with stars, Esta and I fall asleep at once.

In the morning I feel sick when I'm led into the hut. It's like being swallowed up in a bottle of ink and the messy blackness of it takes my breath away. When my eyes get used to the dark I see a scooped-out pit in the centre of the floor filled with glowing charcoal. An old woman, with dried-up breasts flapping at her waist, squats beside it. She has huge cracked hands and wears a greasy leather apron. It slaps against her wizened thighs as she fans the embers with a chipped plate.

There's a world here that can't be seen, like the world in dark sleep or the one on the other side of a black night sky or beneath the surface of water. The fire burns red, a handful of powdery leaves is thrown on to the flames and rancid smoke curls round the hut and makes my eyes sting. I cough and try to turn away but Mama's hands are resting firmly on my shoulders. A second woman, with a polio leg all twisted and soft like maize porridge, starts to beat out a rhythm with sticks on a metal bowl; quietly at first, then louder and more insistent till the clattering of wood on tin makes shivers run across my skin.

Suddenly I'm pushed to the floor. Someone smelling of stale fat pins my arms to the ground, another jerks my legs apart and the old witch peers between them as if I was a gutted fish laid open for inspection in the market. With a knife she slices into my flesh. There's a smell like iron and I feel hot rushing liquid between my legs as if I've wet myself. Then pain. I howl and Mama clamps her hand over my lips so that the shameful noise will not be heard outside. I bite her strongly on the fleshy root of her thumb and taste salty blood. Mama flinches.

Serves you right. Why didn't you tell me it would be like this? Oh Lord Jesus, is this what being a woman means? You tricked me.

But I can only scream in my head because she keeps her hand pressed down hard on my mouth. I struggle to get away but other hands grip me like cold iron bangles. The old hag is scraping at me with a piece of broken glass. I kick out, hitting some hard bony part of her. She gasps. A moment's relief. The scraping starts again. Then I am darned together and doused in disinfectant.

I cannot walk. Mama carries me to a hut to recover with the other girls. This is sorrow food and I cry without making a noise. In a dark, tangled, needful way I can't quite understand why I want Mama more at this moment than I have ever done. But she does not come. Only the crone and her followers come. I hear Esta's voice.

'Rozina,' she whispers and we lie alongside each other, fingertips touching for comfort.

I bleed. I keep bleeding – like the drops falling from the Sacred Heart of Jesus on the statue in Church, the colour of the bishop's cape or the lipstick of the bar girls at the Hollywood Inn. Is that why they're called scarlet women? Did they have this done to them? Mama says men like scarlet women. But they only go with them, don't marry them. That's what she says. That's what this is about, getting married, being respectable.

'I would rather be a scarlet woman than go through this' I croak to Esta and she nods.

Our mamas enjoy the days spent without the responsibilities of families. In this place where the hot stinging smell of the bush lingers in the air like cooking-fire smoke, they gossip, make up jokes, tell stories and murmur about old scandals.

They lied to me. They all lied to me, my father, my mother. My sister lied with her silence. It hurts.

I have a fever. I ache all over and my throat is dry as sand. I am scorched and light, so light I think I might float away. I see strange birds in the patterns of the tree branches, and the faces of the girls and women around me look like the faces of elephants and hyenas. I watch them swell up, large and round, then grow tiny as a grain of maize. Mama nurses me until fat drops of sweat burst out of my skin and trickle down my body so that the blanket under me is as wet as if it had fallen in the river. I need help to walk back to the pick-up point for the bus.

When we get home Mama lays me on a mattress on the floor.

'Why?' I ask.

'Custom and tradition,' my mama says.

I don't think this is a proper answer.

'Why?' I ask again.

'Pleasure is for men,' she says, 'for women, there are babies'.

Again I ask, 'Why?'

Mama shrugs her shoulders. She has no other answer. It makes no sense to me. Why do women do this to other women? Why do mothers do this to their daughters? Why does my father allow it?

It's two weeks before I can go back to school. I stop playing football with the boys on the baked earth pitch and my father turns down nine head of cattle, a goat and ten thousand shillings offered by a government official for me to become his second wife. My parents argue about this.

'Rozina's too young,' my mama says.

But not too young for the other thing.

Pain changes the shape of your face. Now, when I look in the shiny scoured base of a pot I can see that my cheeks are no longer round and the skin is stretched tightly across my bones. My eyes look different too. Glassy, like my sister's.

In bed at night, my hand creeps between my legs. All gone. Nothing there but hard crusty scabs and the knotted end of the thread the butchering crone used to stitch me together. It tugs and burns as the wound closes. But where is the soft moist bud that I used to rub with my finger? What happened to those pieces of my flesh that were cut away? What happened to the unfolding flowers behind the hair growing at the top of my legs, the ones that blossomed each morning when I tickled the warm tender pucker of skin between my thighs?

Pain and loneliness ooze up around me like river mud.

I will never let them do this to my daughters. Never.

ELIZABETH KAY
Cassie

She's playing now. I watch her, the way her dark head tilts as she talks to her farm animals, telling them what they're doing as she shuffles them across the floor. I did wonder whether to get her the plastic models; they're more realistic. But in the end I decided against it – the pre-war lead ones are perfectly adequate, better in some ways. I know their contours, the solid feel they have in the palm of your hand. I owned a set of them when I was a boy. Her pig has a missing leg, and her cow has a moon-shaped dent in its side. All good stuff when you're playing the vet game. The paint's poisonous, of course, and it does peel off. She licks her finger. You can worry about that if you like.

She's an attractive child; I find it rather surprising that no one wanted her. Eyes the colour of Belgian chocolate, skin liked iced coffee, hair so black I am tempted to ascribe a liquorice shine to it. A lively, slightly asymmetrical face with a bumpy nose. Maybe she's not conventional enough for an age in which superficial appearance is everything. Her appeal is more than skin deep, you see. Her voice has a bossy little edge to it, her gestures are quick and expressive, she has an enquiring mind. At the moment she's asking a chicken why it's coloured white, because white isn't very good camouflage in a farmyard unless it's snowing. She knows about protective colouration – she would do, wouldn't she?

All her clothes came from a charity shop. A bit threadbare, here and there, but perfectly serviceable. The shoes were the trickiest – it was difficult to find ones that fitted, and in the end I had to cut out the toes because she kept on getting blisters. But she doesn't seem to feel the cold the way I do; goose-pimples don't bother her. She loves the white cotton dress with the poppies on it. They look like splashes of blood from a distance.

I've called her Cassandra; a Greek name, originally, so it seemed appropriate. The Greek border wasn't all that far away from where she was born, in what was called Yugoslavia at the time. Her English is pretty good now – only the faintest trace of an accent when she's upset about something, or excited, or tired. A few grammatical errors, but not many. She still sucks her thumb, but it's only to be expected.

I ought to find out a bit more about her I suppose, but I don't like to ask. I only have the haziest picture of her parents, but it's probably enough. Sometimes research throws up things you don't want to know, things that are better let be, things that side-track you from the real issues. But I'm not sure that we live in a world of real issues any more – just cosmetic ones, fabricated ones, the ones that lend themselves to tick-lists and exclusion policies.

On one occasion I took her to the Oxford University Museum of Natural History. There was a perfectly good reason for it – it's still a museum, not a succession of flashing lights and buttons and levers, designed for the three-minute attention span. She liked the stuffed birds, and the insect collection, and she looked at the triceratops skeleton for a long time. Then she said, 'Is that bullet-hole? Did someone shoot it?'

'*A* bullet-hole,' I corrected her. Then I explained about the structure of the skull, the openings for blood vessels and nerves, and pointed out that there was an identical hole on the other side.

'Yes,' she said thoughtfully, 'it *is* exactly same size, so it can't be exit wound.'

'*The* same size, and *an* exit wound,' I admonished – not because I enjoyed finding fault with her, but because it was necessary. 'Guns hadn't been invented when this creature was alive. It's a dinosaur.'

'I thought dinosaur – *a* dinosaur – was a political party,' she said. 'One that can't adapt to change.'

You see? No one liked the way she spoke, too precocious, too strange, too untutored in the ways of the consumer society. I showed her the dodo, and acquainted her with the story of its extinction. She didn't seem surprised that something could be wiped out so thoughtlessly. Then I gave her the theory of evolution, and went into some detail about adaptation and survival of the fittest. I observed in passing that these days natural selection has frequently been replaced by *un*natural selection. Dobermans and Pekineses, Shires and Shetlands. But her eyes lit up when I told her there was a time when men did not exist.

'I wish I could have been alive then,' she said.

'Your place is with the future,' I told her. 'That's why you're called Cassandra.'

'The trouble with being Cassandra,' she said, 'is that no one ever takes any notice.'

And, of course, she was right. Perhaps I should change her name. Perhaps that *was* why no one listened. On the other hand, perhaps I'm just not very good at names.

So I took her to The Natural History Museum in London, and we pushed all the buttons and pulled all the levers and watched all the video clips. I didn't enjoy it; everything smelt of plastic, not preserving fluids and old books, and my disaffection probably came across. The place was packed, and we ate our lunch surrounded by noisy children playing games on mobile phones.

Cassandra leaned across to look.

'Sod off,' said a small boy with red hair, 'you've just made my snake crash.'

'Cars crash,' she said. 'Snakes squelch.'

He looked interested all of a sudden. 'You've got a squelch sound, not a beep? Cool.'

'I trod on an asp once.'

'A what?'

'An asp.'

He looked irritated for a moment, trying to wrench the name from his memory. I saw his mouth form the word Cleopatra. Then he sneered and said, 'Yeah, like you get asps in England.'

'It wasn't *in* England. I didn't see it; asps have cryptic camouflage. It made a sort of popping sound, and then it squelched.'

'Pull the other one.'

'Like treading on a tangerine. You hear the skin split first.'

'Liar.'

Cassandra deftly took the phone from him and smiled as he clutched at thin air. Then she said, 'What sort of noise do you think this would make if I trod on it?'

The boy flew at her, fists and ginger curls everywhere, and his mother leaped to her feet and dragged them apart. I looked the other way, but I heard her say, 'Give him back his phone. *Now*. What were you going to do, sell it? I can see what you are – one of those grubby little travellers. Those tatty clothes, the hair, the eyes. I've a good mind to report you.'

'Why?' said Cassandra. 'I didn't actually do anything. Or doesn't that matter?'

'Cheeky little brat,' said the woman. There was a squeal as she presumably seized her son by the arm, and I heard their footsteps click away across the stone floor.

When we got home Cassandra said, 'I've been called that before. A traveller. It's another word fro gypsy, isn't it?'

'Does it bother you?'

'It might make things easier if I looked more like everyone else,' she said.

I don't want you to think I don't care about her – I do, desperately. So I'm going to bleach her hair and get her some new clothes.

She does look different blonde. And she's washing her face every day – I'm not sure I approve, I rather liked the smudges on her cheeks – wisps of smoke, echoes of gunfire. She's made me get her a toothbrush and some shower-gel. She still doesn't think she looks pretty enough, though. I tell her being pretty isn't all it's cracked up to be, but she says I've got it wrong.

That she needs to fit in. Fit in with what, I say. People's expectations, she says. People would be nicer to me if I were pretty. And then, perhaps, they'd start to listen.

I'm not sure I've made the right choice with a Bosnian child. I liked the association with the six children who saw visions of the Virgin, warning of troubles to come. Plenty of people took their predictions seriously, but not those who counted. Not those who could have stopped what happened after. The trouble with visions is that they're a bit too supernatural. A bit too minority interest. A bit too pull the other one. Of course, Cassandra isn't actually one of the six who saw the Virgin – she just comes from the same area. Prophecy by association. Don't spell it out, don't hit them with a sledgehammer, make them work a little. But what do you do when you've been right, over and over again, and no one takes a blind bit of notice?

Adapt, I suppose. Adapt.

She wants me to call her Cassie. Cassandra's too long, she says, and it sounds pretentious and out of date. And she's really worried about her nose. She says it doesn't look like anyone else's, it's all bumpy, like a switchback; she wants plastic surgery. I tell her she's too young, but she says I can do anything, can't I? I don't like to tell her I can't – otherwise we wouldn't be in this mess – but I chicken out. I'm not ready for feet of clay. So Cassie gets her plastic surgery and an Elizabeth Taylor nose.

I've had to send her to school. I didn't want to, for all sorts of reasons, but in the end I had no choice. And she *has* made a friend. A redhead called Sharon, who has problems at home. They play with the farm animals for hours on end, building smallholdings out of cereal packets and toilet rolls and constructing stooks from dried grass. The stooks are Cassie's idea, of course. Sharon wouldn't know a stook if it hit her in the face – the only hay she's ever encountered was seen from a car window, baled by a machine and wrapped in black plastic. I'm none too sure about Sharon, I think she might be a bad influence. There's a knowing look in those baby blue eyes that I don't like – it's quite different from Cassie's patchy worldliness, which is coupled with a sweet beguiling innocence. In Sharon's hands the bull and the cow get up to all sorts of things; I'm keeping a firm eye on the farmer and the sheep, though as yet there's no intimation of intimacy.

Cassie's come home late from school, in tears. Her curly blonde hair is streaked with mud, her trainers are coated with it. I tell her it's just superficial, let them dry and it'll crack off, like the shell of a hard-boiled egg.

'That's not it,' she sniffs, wiping her pert little nose with a tissue. She used to wipe it on her sleeve – I think I preferred it that way.

'So what is it?'

'Why does no one believe me?' she wails. 'We were doing a project on famine, so I told my teacher what it's like to be hungry. *Really* hungry, when your stomach cramps up and your head feels as though it could float away and leave your body behind, and you wish it would. Then Sharon said I make up all sorts of things, like my parents being shot, and the teacher said that was a wicked thing to say, and she gave me a detention.'

Cassie's parents had been shot? I hadn't known that. Not until now, anyway.

'And there was a whole gang of them waiting for me when I came out, and they kept calling me a liar. They pushed me in the mud and said if half what I said was true I ought to have scars all over my body, and nightmares, and be behind at English.'

I won't have anyone criticise Cassie's English. Not now. She's a very bright girl and children pick up languages amazingly quickly.

'There's no reason for you to be bad at English,' I say. 'We don't have a television, and you spend a lot of time reading.'

'I come top in all the spelling tests. Should I get things a bit more wrong, do you think?'

'Certainly not,' I tell her. There are some things that just aren't negotiable.

She's playing with her farm animals again, but this time their injuries are caused by mortar shells and incendiary bombs. She says that's what's needed. I think it's all a bit melodramatic, personally. I'm pretty sure it's Sharon who's encouraging her – the little minx watches all sorts of highly unsuitable things on the television.

Cassie's had a nightmare. People running, smoke, screams that turn to gurgles and die away. She's frightened. She's hiding in a farmhouse, but the house doesn't have a roof any more, and she can see the flames shooting up from the barn and making faces at her in the sky. She wants her mother, but her mother has become a sack of potatoes, and the soldiers want to roast them in the ashes and there's no way she can stop them, so she runs away. It's snowing, but every snowflake burns her, and she's stippled with little red marks, the measles of war. She knows these marks will identify her, so she dyes her hair blonde and cuts off her nose.

She says that when she woke up she didn't know where she was, and I'm not sure I do either. Is this going to become a regular occurrence? She says she's never going to eat a potato again, which will make dinner tricky. Oh, it's easy to be flippant. I must control it.

She's toying with her food. I made her a good breakfast today – though to be honest I'm not too fussed about regular meals, they can end up dominating things. Fruit – she likes that, there wasn't much of it where she came from, not in the winter, at any rate. Bacon, tomatoes, mushrooms. She doesn't think our supermarket mushrooms have much flavour – she used to gather ceps and truffles and chanterelles. She glances up at me. There's a new look in those dark eyes, a faint scepticism. As though all of a sudden she's wondering how fallible I might be. She considers me a moment longer, then she says, '*Other people* can't see my nightmares, can they? I need the scars.'

I don't like this.

'A few cigarette burns, maybe, and a knife wound. You should use something with a serrated edge, so that it leaves more evidence.'

I shake my head.

'It won't take long.'

I know that.

'It might be nice to arrange the burns so that they form some initials.'

'Kilroy was here?'

'Don't be flippant, Amos.'

From the other side of the table I study her skin. The smooth unbroken surface of a cup of café au lait, the faint gleam, the uniformity of it. She's like that all over; too young for body hair, too old for second thoughts. She opens my packet of cigarettes and lights one. It doesn't look right. She blows a smoke-ring with surprising expertise. That doesn't look right, either. Then she hands me the cigarette and rolls up her sleeve.

I don't want to do it. I really don't. When the glowing tip touches her skin she doesn't flinch. There's a soft hissing sound, and a brief smell of barbecue. I move a little further to the right and do it again. The same sound, the same smell. She doesn't even whimper. I carry on until I've written A.V. on her forearm.

'You didn't have to sign your own initials, silly,' she says.

'Yes I did.'

She gives me an old-fashioned look, gets up and fetches the bread-knife. Feels the edge with her fingertip. Nods with satisfaction. Points to her cheek.

'No. Not your face.'

She's a bit disappointed in me, I can see that. But she isn't going to argue – she knows a lost cause; she's seen far too many of them. She slides her school skirt up her thigh, it's navy blue, pleated, as dark as a night sky. She indicates the inside of her leg.

'No. I might sever the femoral artery.'

'*Have* you ever killed anyone?'

I don't want to answer that. She offers me the other side of her thigh, and I close my eyes and cut.

'Don't do it like that, you coward. You can't do the job properly if you don't put everything into it.'

I open my eyes, and saw with the blade. I feel faint. This

isn't what I wanted at all, but I've got to do it the way she says. Double-think. Somehow. When the leg is sufficiently mutilated she nods, and I fetch a towel and try to stop the bleeding. It seems to go on for a long time.

She heals fast – too fast, really. As do I, it seems. I look at those initials from time to time, but they don't have the impact they did. I've become hardened to them. I know the school won't do anything about the scars – as far as they're concerned, she's always had them.

Sharon is round again. They've abandoned the farm, and they're trying out make-up in the bathroom. I'd like to tell Sharon to sling her hook, but I suspect we need her. She's streetwise, contemporary, a touch of the here and now. She swears, of course, and she bunks off school to play doctors and nurses with the boys from the comprehensive. I know far more than I'd like to about her background – her mother's an alcoholic, and her father indulges in a smörgasbord of violence on Saturday nights. Sharon will probably become a prostitute, although that isn't really my concern.

Sharon wants Cassie to go to a disco with her, but I'm drawing the line at that. I know nothing about discos, and I'm damned if I'm going to find out.

She glares at me. 'Sharon says I should get a life.'

'You've got one, Cassie.'

'One that *you* orchestrate. I know fuck all about music.'

The swear-word is a shock. 'We'll listen to some Mahler,' I say.

'*Mahler*. I don't think so.'

'Debussy?'

'Oh sure, that's really cool.'

'Philip Glass, then. He's modern.'

'Get real,' she says, and goes to her room.

She can't become a teenager yet, she's not old enough.

Another nightmare. And another. They don't seem to upset her, though – not the way I'd have expected. 'You don't understand me really, do you?' she says.

'Of course I do,' I tell her. 'You're my Cassandra.'

'I *was* your Cassandra,' she says. 'Once.'

There's a bitter taste in my mouth, and a sick feeling in my stomach. I've gone too far. On the other hand, she thinks I still haven't gone far enough.

'The scars are so-so,' she says. 'But they're not really dramatic enough. Sex and violence. No one pays much attention to anything else.'

'No sex,' I say. 'You're too young.'

'Yes,' she says, 'I think you're right on that score.' And just for a moment she's the old Cassandra again, wise beyond her years, unblemished, adorable. A wave of nostalgia overcomes me, and I'm crying. I can't stop – not for a while, anyway. It's quite embarrassing.

'You are an old silly,' she says eventually. 'You take everything far too seriously. You can't change the world, you know, it changes itself.'

'Can't I try?'

'Of course you can *try*. It's in your nature. The Doberman and the Pekinese are still dogs underneath, aren't they? They still get annoyed at the same things.'

'One barks; the other yaps.'

'Yap, then. Someone may hear us. And that means going further still. Further than surface alterations.'

'How much further *can* I go?'

'I asked you whether you'd ever killed anyone.'

No. Stop this now.

'Well? Have you?'

'Yes.'

'How many?'

'Ten, eleven. I don't know. I haven't counted.'

'Count.'

'Eleven. No, twelve.'

'So I'd make thirteen.'

'No way. Forget it.'

'I don't mind. Honestly.'

'Well *I do*.'

'Let's make the final cut.'

'I told you, no.'

'Just kidding, Amos. Finishing me off isn't the object of the exercise – what you really need to do is to amputate something.'

I stare at her. '*What?*'

'An arm, a leg. A finger's not big enough.'

'Haven't we done enough?'

'No. You know we haven't. Right – you're going to need a book on anatomy this time. I know you've got one, *and* you've got some surgical instruments.'

She's absolutely right. I'd borrowed them from a friend when I was researching something, and failed to return them. They were probably slightly out of date, or Doug wouldn't have lent them to me. He'd made no attempt to get them back, anyway.

Something inside me is recoiling already. This is going to be the worst of all.

'I wish I had some anaesthetic,' I say.

'You don't get a local when you have your foot blown off by a mine,' she replies.

I pour myself a whisky, and down it in one. Pour myself another.

'Two's quite enough,' says Cassie. 'You can't work properly if you're pissed.'

I scowl and finish my drink. Then I set to work on her knee. I follow the procedure laid down in the book, carefully, meticulously even. She makes no sound – just watches me with those liquid chocolate eyes of hers, her brows furrowing slightly as a purely objective interest is aroused. I work swiftly, with a deftness of touch I never knew I had. Slicing neatly through the skin, cutting the tendons, parting the bones – the femur, the tibia, the patella. I suture all the blood vessels, and I do it so well that there's very little blood. Not a bad job, actually. You'd almost think her leg had always ended at the knee.

'Well,' she says when I've finished, 'that's it then.'

'You're happy now?'

'*Happy?* No, Amos Vincent, of course I'm not, but that wasn't the point. How would you like to be a pre-pubescent one-legged bottle blonde with someone's initials burnt into your arm? Highly appropriate initials, when you think about it. The Authorised Version. But you've done the job, and I've survived. Time to say goodbye, I think.'

I'd forgotten all about that side of it.

'Oh cheer up,' she says. 'Think about that nice fat cheque.'

I try thinking about it. At the moment, it doesn't help.

'Look,' she says, 'I know you reckon you've sold out. But at least this one's going to get made. You've written storyline after storyline, and had them all rejected. And they were *good* stories – they just told people things they didn't want to hear. You wrote me a long time ago, and no one wanted me. A European war, they said? Pull the other one. And now along comes a spanking new TV company and says, *adapt this the way we want. Make her a cute little heroine, the victim of more obvious violence, and we've got a deal.* Better to be out there yapping than barking in a cellar where no one can hear, surely?'

Maybe. Maybe not.

HANNAH MCGILL

Praxis and the Human Band-Aid

You won't remember this, but someone had to fuck the superheroes.

And I'm not talking about the pouty, pretty creatures they used to pose with in public, the Lois Lanes and Mary-Janes. Those dames were just for show. They'd have broken in half, believe me, right at their Miss Dior wasp waists. It took a special kind of female to act as blotting paper for all the excess otherworldly testosterone superheroes could exude. Think about it – if you could bend iron rivets with your bare hands, lift trucks to free whimpering infants and scale tall buildings in a single leap, would you be satisfied by a quick bout of orthodox in-out activity? No way. Furthermore, the satisfaction of the superheroes was considered a national security issue. If their tiny little brains were marinating in untapped sexual energy, and their tights were all clogged up with unshot loads, they might not be able to focus on the job in hand. They were liable to start busting up foreign embassies and dropping well-dressed men in reservoirs just to work off some tension.

Which is where we came in. They called us superhookers – but personally I found that a little derogatory, considering the delicate and significant nature of our work. We were employees of the government (that's right – the President was my pimp). So we were clean, we were licensed, and we were highly, highly trained. We had to be. Could a superhero trust any chick off the street, not only to take on a physique designed for vanquishing evil in all its forms, but also to stay the hell away from the press afterwards? Way back, the gutter press used to heave with ill-dressed sluts crowing about nights of passion with the Hulk, or the Silver Surfer, or some intriguing combination of X-Men. And you can bet your little ass that two-thirds of those dumb girls ended up in jacuzzis with supervillains, being promised plastic surgery in exchange for names and numbers. When they regulated the system and clamped down on fraternisation with civilians, those girls went right back to fucking movie stars and senators, which was safer for everyone – including them. A horny superhero was no easy ride, if you'll pardon the turn of phrase. I used to keep a tiny nub of Kryptonite in my purse to slow Superman down when he got too enthusiastic. It wasn't just the brute strength, either. When Spiderman got excited, those sticky webs would fly out of him every which way; I went through every drycleaner in town trying to shift the residue. And anyone who's had an ice-cream headache can imagine the painful legacy of going down on Iceman.

Not that they were all glamour boys, you understand. There were always plenty of low-ranking superheroes who didn't get a lot of press attention. Most of them did standard kid-in-a-well jobs, although there were those whose skills were more specific. Consider if you will the very bottom of the pile: Mr Thesaurus, who dealt with synonym emergencies, or

Bonus Man, who alerted shoppers to special offers they might not otherwise have noticed. That type of superhero was pretty much like an ordinary guy, except he could go a little longer and contact Washington through his wristwatch. They were nice, actually – still grateful, which was more than you'd ever get from some swell-chested prima donna who had his own press office and put out a calendar every year.

No-one would believe it now, but I really did take pride in my job. I was one of the best. They'd ask for me by name. Special occasion? Call Praxis. As you can probably imagine, the superheroes used to absorb some pretty retro ideas about male/female relations – if you had a pair of tits, you might as well have been tied to a railtrack – so they favoured voluptuous, feminine girls. Back then my figure was a licence to print money.

Still, by the time I met The Human Band-Aid, I was starting to feel like time was firmly on someone else's side. When the phone rang that fateful day, I was standing naked in front of the full-length mirror, assessing the damage. I used to do that a lot – and every time there were a few more pounds on my haunches and a few more dimples on my thighs. Part of my appeal was always my genuine D-cup silicone-frees, but they'd started to look as if they could do with some surgical enhancement. I wasn't feeling too encouraged as I reached for the receiver.

'Miss Murgatroyd? Hilly. I'm delighted to say I have a very special assignment for you.'

'How are you, Hilly? It's been a while.'

'Yes it has, Miss Murgatroyd. Can I tell you your assign-ment?'

'Please do. I was about ready to heal up over here.'

'Quite. We'd like you to accompany The Human Band-Aid to tomorrow night's function, if you think you could.'

'I think I *could*. But tomorrow night? Isn't he—'

'Oh yes. And you're his date. You won the jackpot. There will be media attention so be sure to dress appropriatcly. Meet his assistant at the Lopsthorne Hotel at nineteen hundred hours, please. She will handle all the details. There's just one other thing, Miss Murgatroyd.'

'Yes?'

'I've been reviewing the records and you don't seem to be very up to date with your Psych tests.'

'Oh . . . really? Did I miss one?'

'Try three, Miss Murgatroyd. I've scheduled one for you tomorrow at nine a.m. and if you don't show, you can consider yourself on suspension.'

'OK. Got it. Um – any special requirements for the Band-Aid guy?'

'He prefers low heels. Goodbye.'

'Never less than a pleasure, Hilly.'

We had monthly psychiatric examinations, along with sexual health check-ups, pregnancy tests and weigh-ins. I told you the government took our work seriously, didn't I? They monitored our bust measurements; they demanded to know our dreams. Well, it made sense: some of the stuff we had to deal with was pretty weird, and there was a certain degree of emotional loop-the-loop. Also, and more importantly as far as they were concerned, they had to make sure we weren't dabbling in the dark side. Any hint that one of their girls had a mild attraction to weapons, or a fascination for Russian guys with big pointy eyebrows, and she'd be off the job quicker than The Amazing One-Minute Man.

Most of us didn't particularly like taking the Psych tests. The older you get, the less comfortable it is whipping out your dirty laundry. I knew I would have to come up with something pretty good to avoid that morning appointment, but first of all, I had to call Vermillion and tell her about my date.

'Honey! The guy with the healing hands? I was just reading about him in Pex magazine. He is such a cutie! And tomorrow night's gonna be big for him, from what I hear.'

'Sure is. Not bad for an old broad, huh?'

'Sweetie, don't even. You know you're fabulous. All those little twenty-year-olds with their boob jobs and braces will be spitting mad when they hear about this. This is gonna put you right back on the frontline.'

'That's if Hilly can restrain herself from putting my ass on suspension.'

'Suspension? *You*? Why the fuck? That would be like suspending . . . the Queen from Buckingham Palace! What did you do?'

'I missed a couple of Psych tests.'

Vermillion took a breath. 'Is this about what I think it's about? You have to let it go. It's so fucking dangerous. Remember what happened to Gloria Globes.'

There was a moment of silence as we both contemplated Gloria Globes, a legend among our number until she got taken hostage by Dr Despicable and quickly decided he wasn't quite so despicable after all. Following a ten-day stand-off at his cave in the mountains, Gloria and the bad Doctor came out to face the world, and died hand-in-hand under a confetti storm of FBI bullets.

'I won't do a Gloria, Milly. This is just a glitch.'

'I hope so, honey. Be careful. Hell, even the good guys are dangerous right now. I heard that some girl landed up in the hospital with a fractured pelvis thanks to The Battering Ram.'

'God, did she miss a remedial class, or what?'

'I know. Strictly manual and oral attention for guys who specialise in the redirection of hurricanes.'

'I guess I won't have to worry about injuries tonight.'

'Guess not. Think he cures menstrual cramps?'

'I'll ask him.'

The Human Band-Aid was generally acknowledged to be fucking fantastic. He had blond wavy hair, like some kind of dandy Chaucerian knight, and fat caramel muscles bulging under his suggestive flesh-tone costume. He could also knit together ruptured skin with a single touch of his big knotty hands, which is a fine addition to anyone's resumé. And every snitch in town was spreading the word that the following night he would be named New Face Of The Year at the annual dinner and awards ceremony held by the Federal Board of Extra-Human Order-Promoting Superpeople. (The word 'crime-fighting' was in there originally, but it was dropped due to political pressure to play down the violent aspect of the superheroes' work). This was basically a guarantee of legendary status. From then on, The Human Band-Aid would be getting all the big jobs. His action figure would be on every little boy's Christmas list – and I'd be on his arm!

The future was so damn bright, I had new crow's feet just from squinting at it.

It took me three hours to get ready. I wasn't taking any chances. I knew that if some bitchy gossip columnist caught the glint of a grey hair, or invited readers to phone in and guess my weight, I'd be all washed up by breakfast. So everything loose was strapped down or bolstered up; everything stubbly was plucked bald and polished to a high gloss; everything flaky was richly moistened with heavy-smelling unguents. The dress was kind of retro-ironic – Wonderwoman red and blue with a corset structure and the cutest little cape. I hoped this might help the editors out with their headlines – The New Boy Wonder Meets His Wondergirl – that kind of thing. (Robin would probably sue, but then hardly a day went by without him suing some poor sucker for misusing his trademark or casting aspersions on his pure, noble, platonic bond with his boss.) Seems funny now, but even after (whisper it) twenty-odd years in this line of work, I was still susceptible to the odd romantic fantasy. A spark between myself and Mr Wonderful, a clandestine association spiralling onward through the years. Superheroes weren't supposed to fall in love, of course, but it wasn't unheard of. I mean, Lindy Plantagenet and The Cannonball Kid carried on like a pair of turtle doves for six years, but because they were both considered safe and steady individuals, a blind eye was kindly turned.

My efforts were such that by 18.27 hours, I felt like I could have slain a man at a hundred paces using only my ass. By 19.18, I knew why The Human Band-Aid preferred low heels. Still, by 21.40, munchkin or not, he was officially New Face Of The Year. By 02.15, the face of the New Face Of The Year was between my thighs. And by 02.21, his dick was curled up in my hand like a sleepy baby rattlesnake, and his tears were causing some unsightly buckling on the surface of my Linda Carter shoulder pads.

'You're *crying*? But you guys don't . . . you can't . . .'

'I know, goddamnit! We're not supposed to cry and we're sure as hell not supposed to be . . .'

'Impotent. I was getting to that.'

'It's all such *bull*!'

He succumbed to a fresh fit of sobbing, and I gently shifted his head off my dress. We were in his hotel room, which would have been a truly beautiful confection of gossamer drapes, calla lilies and embroidered pillowslips, if he hadn't tipped his belongings out all over the floor like a disgruntled teen on laundry day, and kicked a hole in the bathroom wall. He was younger than I had expected, and much less handsome; his front teeth poked forward like little arrowheads and he had a lazy eye. He was acting kind of drunk. He'd had his fair share of champagne at the awards, but that shouldn't have been an issue: under normal circumstances, it took a tankerload of tequila to get a superhero tipsy. As for the dick thing, that was just bizarre. Sorry to be crude and all, but I hadn't had a penis resist my attentions in seventeen years (not since Vladimir The Corroder poisoned Pantherboy and he started to die while I was blowing him). I'd forgotten what a flaccid one felt like – that weird, chewed-gum texture, that helpless, beseeching droop.

'What do you think is wrong?' I gently asked him, before remembering that I was a hooker, not a therapist, and adding, 'Maybe if I took off the dress?'

'No, don't Praxis . . . DON'T!' he retorted with insulting zeal. 'You think you could just lie here a bit and talk to me? I don't get to talk to anyone.' Sensing my reluctance, he made a judicious appeal to my avarice. 'C'mon . . . you're getting paid, aren't you? What have you got to lose?'

So I got two beers from the minibar, drew the starchy lavender-scented counterpane around me, and tried not to let my wounded pride spoil this special night of ours. I sure as hell didn't want to leave without some credible explanation for his failure to perform. Otherwise I knew I would spend the next three days crying into the bathroom scale.

'What is it that's such bull?' I began, in my best nurturing voice. He made the face of a small boy staring into the sun, and gestured as if to say: it's too much, too voluminous to ever express.

'*All* of it,' he said. 'The whole damn racket. Having to do this. It's all totally fake – you must know that? Hell, two hours after I pose for pictures with some Indonesian arms dealer in a headlock, he's having cocktails on the White House lawn. It's all for show – they just put us up front to distract the public while they get on with the usual bribery and corruption behind the scenes. We're decoys is all. Decoys in fuckin' ugly leotards.' He snorted back phlegm and took a deep pull of beer. I've got to admit, at this point I was shocked. It's not like I was ever the most patriotic kid in the class, but there are some things you rarely hear spoken out loud, and in my twenty years of fucking superheroes, no-one had voiced this type of shit. Everyone knew there were crackpot theorists out there, who swore that superheroes were actually enemy agents, or government stooges, or even emissaries of Satan. But most rational folks didn't give credence to those stories. I mean, there's enough evil in the world to get worked up about, isn't there, without turning your anger and suspicion against guys who are expressly designed to do good?

'It can't be a bad thing, though,' I implored him, 'to have healing powers. How can that be a bad thing?'

'That in itself is not a bad thing,' he said, wrapping the hotel robe around him and flopping down next to me on the bed. 'It's great. It was great when I first started, before anyone knew, out in the country . . . I used to zap my own cuts and bruises, mend baby birds' legs, help my mom with her migraines. But as soon as someone reported me to the Board, that was it. I was a government resource. Every move I've made since then has been strictly regulated. From who I fight to what I eat.'

It used to be that if someone you knew exhibited signs of superpowers, you had a legal obligation to report it to the Board. Knowingly harbouring a suspected superhero was a pretty serious offence. Then again, why would anyone want to hide that kind of talent, right?

'But they're so good to you. And everyone loves you. Everyone wants to be a superhero,' I said. I was suffering Santa Claus levels of disillusionment.

'Sure, they give us all this money, status, chicks.' He indicated me, and I felt slightly pleased to be counted as a perk. 'But it's just so that we'll stay docile. Sure, most of the guys dig it. They're young and they're vain and it's good fun, you know? Putting on a big show, getting your picture taken all the damn time. It's not like it's a bad life.'

'But?'

'But it's fake as shit. We've got no choice. It's not like I get a distress call and make up my own mind to fly out to do good. I get a call and I get told where to be and when.'

'Just like me,' I marvelled.

'I guess. We're in the same game.'

Both of us thought this over for a time. We were cosied up like children and I suddenly thought: If I'd had a brother it might have felt like this. Hansel and Gretel. Praxis and The Human Band-Aid.

'What's your real name?' I asked him.

'Lyle.'

I lay back on the bed, a little drunk, a little blown away by what Lyle had said. It had never struck me that superheroes could get cynical too. It seemed OK to tell him anything now. So I yawned and said, 'I've got stretch marks on my tits and I haven't even had a baby. Now THAT's a fucking injustice. Why don't you channel all those energies of yours into stopping nature from draining me of my livelihood?'

He sighed deeply, and took me a little more seriously than I had intended. 'We can't do that stuff, Praxis. You know we can't. Moving trains, sure; nuclear warheads, maybe. But not *time*. I can't stop time. I can't make you more beautiful.'

'You don't think I'm beautiful enough?'

'Oh, Christ. I thought the whole attraction of hookers was that they didn't come out with that kind of shit.'

'No, dear – the attraction of hookers is that you get to fuck them any which way you please, and that seems to present something of a problem, so quit coming on like you're some fucking wise old stud.'

We looked at each other and then we laughed. It was nice; I didn't know when I'd last lain in bed with a man and not fucked him, let alone laughed with him. I got another beer. He glanced at the clock by the bed and made a whining sound.

'Tomorrow at ten I have an appointment to kick ass. It'll be the biggest thing I've ever done and I don't want to do it.'

'Who's the lucky villain?'

'The biggest one of all. The Cuddles.'

We'd established this weird, uninhibited rapport, and I guess I couldn't prevent the blush from seeping all over my face and neck. He cocked an eyebrow. The thing is, he'd just hit on my equivalent of Kryptonite. The Cuddles: my secret weakness. My Achilles heart. The Cuddles is a major Mafioso, so named because he was built like a brick snowman, and he'd been known to hug people to death. He's six foot six, three hundred pounds, with arms like legs and a puffy, beat-up boxer's face. And ever since our eyes had met across the carnage during a standoff between his gang and my date a year before, not an hour had gone by that I hadn't thought of him.

'Praxis. What's going on?'

I don't know why I trusted Lyle, but somehow I couldn't or didn't want to lie.

'The Cuddles is my big secret, Lyle. I'm in love with him. It's ruining everything for me. It could cost me my job. Could cost me everything, if they find out.'

Lyle was looking at me quizzically, processing this. 'I guess you've noticed . . . the way he smells.'

Like cigars and gunpowder and horse sweat. 'Yeah, I know.'

'And the size of him.'

Six foot six, three hundred pounds. I look like the Sugar-plum Fairy next to him.

'Yeah.'

'And those rings under his eyes like he's got a liver complaint. And the fact that he's purest, distilled evil.'

'I know, OK? I know it's weird. But everyone has someone they can't resist, even if it's totally wacko and illogical. I can't help it. And I know he feels it too. Sometimes I'll see him someplace, at the back of a bar, or cruising in some fancy armoured vehicle, and something just zings between us like static electricity. He cancels out every other man I've ever met.'

'And that's a lot of men.'

'Fuck you, Elastoplast boy.'

So, that's how it happened. That's how Praxis Murgatroyd, superhooker, missed her fourth compulsory Psych test and wound up on the run, in a Wonderwoman dress, riding shotgun in a borrowed Merc with the New Face Of The Year. Two outlaws with a trunkful of stolen hotel towels (it was his first small act of rebellion – well, his second, after leaving his radar wristwatch on the nightstand). The deal was that The Cuddles and his gang would hold up a major city bank and shoot a couple of clerks. The Human Band-Aid would arrive in the nick of time, put the clerks back together with his magic hands, subdue the gang and await the authorities, all to the tune of rapturous public applause. In reality, Lyle told me, the authorities had planned the whole thing, with the co-operation of their close business associate, The Cuddles. It was a stunt to emphasise how tough they were on malfeasants, to quell any rumours that they were in cahoots with organised crime, and to prove what a worthy use of taxpayer dollars the New Face

Of The Year would be. I was having trouble accepting the fact that all the fights and feats I'd been witness to all these years, all the tales of derring-do I'd cooed over in bed, had been nothing but smoke, snake oil and mirrors – but the minibar booty in the glove compartment kind of softened the blow. Besides, I felt freer than I had in years. I hadn't even combed my hair, or checked for extra chins in the mirror.

When we pulled up outside the Vertigo City Grand Union Bank, we immediately noticed the creepy-looking underlings lurking outside, eyeing the sky for any incoming do-gooders. We had to act fast and slick. We knew the government guys would already be on alert, because Lyle hadn't checked in that day, or responded to any of their calls. I knew Hilly and Vermillion would both be calling me too, so I'd turned my beeper off. Since I'd missed the Psych appointment, I was on suspension anyway – I considered myself off duty. Not that that was going to stop me from using my government-licensed firearm, or brandishing it at least. I'd never had to use it before – even owning it had freaked me out – but now I was ready for anything. I was just rushing like crazy on the adrenaline and the promise of seeing The Cuddles again.

Lyle slid deep down in his seat. I kissed the top of his head, belted my fur tight around my outfit and trotted off up the steps of the bank, trying to look like a normal woman on her way to pay in one of the housekeeping cheques she was saving up in order to take the kids and leave her slob of a husband. As I pushed open the revolving doors I smiled wryly at one of the Board's public information notices – a diagram of puny stick figures ducking respectfully out of the path of a musclebound figure in a fluttering cape, with the words HELP THEM TO HELP US.

I knew The Cuddles was there right away. Before I even saw him, propped against the mortgage advice counter with a copy of the *City Star* held up to his face, I caught that rank circus smell of his, and my heart did a quick flip. No time for lingering glances, though: I knew he was poised to make the signal to his guys. I marched right over and pressed the barrel of my little .45 into his spongy gut. He lowered the paper, with the insouciance of a man who came nose to belly with a gun every day of the working week.

'Praxis Murgatroyd,' he said.

Over the course of a year, these were the first words he'd spoken directly to me. His voice was like a sealion's bark.

'What the fuck?'

'I've gotta tell you, Cuddles,' I purred, as Cuddles' henchmen clocked the situation and started to advance. 'Your gang is looking kinda raggedy. How d'you feel about joining a new one?'

To his guys I called out, 'Keep back – I've got a loaded gun in his stomach.' The cashiers and customers began to panic and race around.

'Are you going to shoot me?' Cuddles asked. I could see the perspiration standing out around his big, broad nose.

'Baby, come with me and I'll shoot you till you beg for more.'

'What do you want?'

'Out of the racket. Don't you?'

The henchmen had formed a semi-circle behind me. The customers and staff had all dropped to the floor, though no-one had told them to. I knew we had a bit of time, since the police would sit tight to give The Human Band-Aid a chance to do his work. I snapped the safety catch. The Cuddles and I looked into one another's eyes until I thought I'd melt all over the marble floor. Alarms were going off, but from where I was at, they sounded like violins. And then one of the henchmen took a chance and blew a bullet right into my lower back. It certainly was a day for new experiences. The shock and impact caused me to pull the trigger on the .45, and Cuddles and I fell together, me howling as loud and shrill as a cat at night, his arms clutching at me, blood pooling between my mink coat and his $6,000 suit.

Out in the car, Lyle The Human Band-Aid heard the shots and knew something had gone wrong. By 09.56, he'd made his heroic entrance and thrown each of the four henchmen into different corners of the bank. The bystanders had picked their heads up off the floor, quit praying and started cheering him on. No-one knew quite what had happened or whose side I was on, but they sure as hell trusted Lyle to do the right thing. More fool them. He laid those warm hands of his on our wounds and I felt all the pain radiate right out of me, like petroleum burning off the surface of a lake. By 10.02, Lyle had carried both of us out to the car – and the alert had gone out all over town that there was a renegade superhero on the run. By 10.27, we were racing away from Vertigo City, Lyle singing at the top of his voice and me locked in a wet smooch with The Cuddles in the back seat. As we crossed the state line, I threw my head back and yelled: 'I'm forty-two!' The Human Band-Aid happily rejoined, 'I'm gay!' And The Cuddles cried, 'I hate the sight of blood!'

* * *

Someone had to fuck the superheroes, like I said. And that's how we did it. By the end of that day, the chairman of the Board had resigned in disgrace, independent factions of self-governing superheroes had sprung up nationwide, and a whole lot of girls in my line of work had woken up and asked themselves whether blow jobs were really part of their patriotic duty.

It's not that things were all bad, the way they were. I mean, the old system held together, a lot of people got rich off it, and I guess at least a couple of rustic peasant hamlets got saved from avalanches. Sure, things are pretty chaotic now that superheroes are unregulated, and they can crop up in the most unlikely places. Plus – needless to say – plenty of the guys stayed right on the government payroll. But now at least we know. We're free. I'll tell you something else, baby, since you've listened so attentively thus far: having a sitter with healing hands made all the difference when you were teething. And we still use those towels.

SYLVIA PEARSON

Bonxie

The wind, a vicious nor-easter with flints of ice in it, tore at the sculpted heath and bogs of the peat-scarred hills, churning lochans, raking rusted reeds, snatching the pungent reek from roadside croft-house lums. Snow on the way. She could smell it, feel its breath stinging the capillaries of her cheeks, whipping them to a tartan redness that no creams or powders could conceal.

Bending into the gale, she tightened her grip on the worn-smooth handles of her wheelbarrow. Another mile and, with God's grace, she would be home with her cargo from the two o'clock launch, a roll of roofing felt for the outhouse, a gallon of paraffin for the lamps, chicken-wire, a slab of yellow Orkney butter for her shop, several pounds of thick biscuits from the mainland bakery and loose tea. She was aye filling up the tea-kist in her shop, a great wooden crate of a thing plastered with labels depicting stooped tea pickers in the plantations of Ceylon: lean smooth-haired women in white or blue cotton saris labouring under a hot sun. Even after all the years of seeing them drying up and curling on the sides of the box, these illustrations, the rich fragrance of tea, could send her off into a dream of exotic lands, and she wondered . . .

But not for long. She would never get off this peerie Shetland island. *Never.*

The thought of a strong brew at the end of her journey urged her on. The working dogs would announce her arrival as soon as she crossed the cattle-grid half a mile from home and Ruby, her sister, would stoke up and set the kettle to a bubbling boil, heat the brown china pot, drop in two cloves and four heaped spoons of tea.

She wore her man-size black beret pulled down over her ears, so she did not hear the scrit and scurry of gravel-crunching footsteps behind her as she turned off onto the hill road, a slight detour path which curved back onto the road again a quarter of a mile ahead. Laurie Williamson had told her at the pier that one of her ewes was limping badly. There would be just enough daylight to discern which one as she had only that morning flitted them to the lower park. She began calling her. All her sheep were individually known to her and answered to pet names: the use of dogs was seldom necessary.

'Sharnie-houghs,' she shouted into the wind, cupping her hands round her mouth. 'Come dee wis, jewel. Sharnie-houghs!' she called in her rich, deep voice. An answering gurgle of bleats came to her from the east corner of the park. She set down her barrow and peered through the fast-falling mirk, and saw the ewe trotting to the fence, lame in a hind leg. Bending low from the waist, she extended a hand through the wires. The wind skelped at her broad back, lifting and flapping the tail of her coat, the bell of her woollen skirt, probing with icy fingers the spaces of naked flesh above her stockings. She put a hand behind her to anchor her clothes and felt it grasped and held fast. The shock of this sent her heart into a wild beating which tightened her chest and took the breath from her. She tried to turn round but her arm had been forced upwards against her spine with terrible force. She could not speak or even cry out. And then a smell came to her, a sickening stench of such power and pervasiveness that her gorge rose. At first, in her panic, she could not put a name to it, but as soon as her assailant began to speak, she knew. Whale oil, from the boiling of blubber in huge vats, a stink far worse than the reek from the gut factory where fish meal was processed, a cloying, belly-churning odour which the whalers from South Georgia could never seem to get rid of, carrying it back in their very pores when they came home on leave. There were two whalers on sick leave on her island. There was only *one* who would do this.

His voice ground words, filthy words, into her ear, his smell laced with the dark molasses cloy of rum and black twist pipe tobacco.

'Got dee at last, my bare-ersed Bonxie. Just dee an me, tagidder alon. Am been waitin a *lang* time fur da taste o dee, lass. Aye, I couldo been a goner. Hidna been for da muckle spikes on me flenser boots, yon winch widda draggit me right ower da stern, but doo canna pit a Tulloch doon for lang, an me strength is comin back. Sees doo, lass, I hae a peerie somethin fur dee, weel, he's no sae *peerie*. Whit tinks doo o *him?*'

He spun her around and she saw that it was indeed Gibbie Tulloch, porcine eyes glittering in the waning light, lips moving wetly in the great bush of black beard. Still he held her by the wrist. His other hand was hauling at his crotch. A bunch of white shirt flapped out and then his long white penis like a death-gasp fish, but rising, rising as he yanked at it until its glistening red eye stared up at her, a pearl of clear fluid trembling like a tear. He was rubber-leg drunk, she could see, but she feared him. He had a *reputation*. Two years ago at a dance in the Hall, she had wrestled away from him and he had threatened to get even. She had laughed away his promises of revenge but had been unable to forget the vile insults he had thrown at her. 'Aye, aye, doo's weel-named Bonxie, big broon bird wi a big roond heid, nae neck tae spik o, an an erse lik an oil tanker. An juist lik da skua, doo feeds aff idder birds' leavins, second-hand feasts o da flesh.'

That her likeness to the arctic skua, pirate of the skies, had earned her this awful nickname she could not argue. The mirror was a thing she looked into for only practical and perfunctory sessions. At the age of thirty she had reconciled herself to life as a single woman, servicing no man, mothering no children. The comfort she found in food had laid on layers of solid flesh. Seeing no reason to decorate or enhance such a body, she wore earth-coloured clothes, *moorit* like some of the caramel-brown Shetland sheep in her flock. But she could not blind herself to the beauty of men's bodies, for it was all around her, a seasonal tapestry of vigour and vitality. Men bent over tushkars in the peat-cutting season, driving shining blades into the treacle-coloured banks, men, often naked to the waist, raking and coling hay, showers of golden flecks flying about their rippling, swinging shoulders, fishermen painting boats, mending nets, heaving and piling their boxes of silver herring. And so this man, this killer of whales with his proud badge, a glinting silver earring, his insult stung and stayed in her heart for she had never, *would* never have messed with a married man.

She found her voice. 'Let go o me flesh, Gibbie Tulloch. Doo's as drunk as a lord wi nane o da refinements. Lay *aff* right dis *meenit* or I'll . . .'

'Doo'll *whit*? Whit'll doo do, Bonxie, lass? Big doo is an strang, but doo'll no git da better o me. Am no haed a wumman for months an am aimin ta pit dat right eenoo, wi *dee*. Doo's ready for it. Am ready for it. Naebody'll ken. It's nature, Bonxie. The coo needs the bull. The bull needs the coo. Lie doon here wi me on dis fine bed o hedder. I'll no hurt dee. Doo'll enjoy it an ax for mair. Here, hae a drap o dis. Hit'll pit fire in dee pussy.'

He pulled a half-bottle of Dark Navy Rum from his jacket pocket, loosened the cap with his teeth and, forcing her head back, rammed it against her mouth. She pursed her lips and the liquid poured down her chin, onto her breasts. Cursing her, he wrenched the bottle away and, mouth agape, glugged the booze down. After watching him gulp the rum almost to emptiness, she fancied that the grip on her wrist had become less vice-like, and although her strong legs had gone weak, as though there was no bone in them, she saw a chance for escape. Wedged in the back of her wheelbarrow was a heavy night-torch. Forcing a softness into her voice, she looked into the rum-reddened eyes of this man.

'Doo'll hae ta let me . . .' she said, indicating below her waist.

He hesitated, eyes translating her gesture, licking his thin, red lips, rocking on his heels, and loosened his hold on her. She made a breenge for the barrow. Her fingers fastened round the cold chrome casing of her torch and she swung it up in a savage arc towards his head. But not nearly quickly enough, and he was on her, a roar of rage strangling in his throat as he drove her to the ground. With a clack of fear, a roosting plover flew up in Gibbie's face, showering its heathery bower with soft breast feathers. Andrina lay, the air forced from her lungs by the fall, gasping and clawing at her breast. With booted feet, he kicked her legs apart and stood looking down at her, face twisted, both hands now yanking feverishly at his fish-belly penis.

'Bitch!' he spat. 'Doo's nearly ruined me herd-on, but no for lang, no for lang.' Somewhere above her flailing head, a *whaap* gave its round-up call, and in her ear she caught the wet bleat of her lame ewe, an echo of her own desolation and despair.

At last some air seeped back into her lungs and she gave a great rattling gasp. With little likelihood of anyone coming along this part of the road, hers was the last croft before the lighthouse, she had no hopes of being rescued. She squeezed her eyes shut when she saw Gibbie push his trousers down to his ankles and bend his knees. He fell on her with a grunt, forcing her hands away from herself and clawing at her woollen knickers and skin with calloused fingers. His weight, his lust were too much for her. He drove into the fjord of her untried flesh and ground at her as if she were a tub of peat-pony mash. Nothing had prepared her for this. His only utterings were foul murmurings in her ear as he plunged like the bull he had earlier spoken of. She was shocked at the pain. How could she, such a broad-hipped woman, have this narrow opening in her body? Biting down hard on her lip, she felt a warm, sticky trickle of blood on her chin. She cried out into the now dark night and heard the answering bleat of her lame ewe. She licked at her lips and the icy wind dried them. Blood and dark rum mingled in her mouth and the acid of bile scalded her throat. She turned her head and vomited on a place by his shoulder, spilling some of the sick on the collar of his coarse, oiled-wool gansey.

She felt the slap and slap of his bare thighs on her own and then a long blast of hot breath on her face as he jerked and humped and finally spent himself inside her. For what seemed an eternity he lay like a log on top of her, his breathing ragged and coarse, the stench of whale oil all around her. At last he withdrew from her and staggered upright. The freezing night air engulfed her and she shivered, teeth chattering, goose-bumps crêping her exposed flesh. She sensed rather than saw the bulk of him straighten against the sky and, rolling over onto her side, curled up into herself.

But someone had seen, had stumbled upon the climax of this scene, had witnessed with pity and horror the violent coupling of this man and woman, the heaving twin moons of the man's buttocks, and had given a strangled cry from spastic vocal cords. But the wind had snatched and swallowed it, and when, through wind-teared eyes, he saw Gibbie Tulloch stagger and head back the way he'd come, he shambled forward from the dry-stane dyke behind which he'd been crouching. The wind buffeted his thin body, threatening to blow him off course as his palsied legs limped him across the road. In his world of silence Dodie Linklater, born deaf, with cerebral palsy, missed very little of what went on on this island, and he hated Gibbie Tulloch with the fierce, uncompromising passion of a child, hated him for the way in which he had stained the memory of his own mother by leaving a once bonny thatched house to the ravages of the elements and the paralysis of neglect. Remembering Ina Tulloch for the gentle woman who had accepted him unconditionally, Dodie knew that she would have been unable to hold her head high in the face of her son's behaviour which had worsened in the eight years since her death.

Gibbie went where his appetites led him, leaving a long line of bastard bairns. That he was the father was not difficult to establish since the infants inevitably bore his unmistakeable stamp, that cow's lick of tarry hair. Additionally, as the whaling season was April to December, time of conception coincided with leave time, thus leaving precious little doubt as to whose seed it was that quickened in the lasses' bellies.

And he was a boaster – 'Aye, it's true I'm a flenser, first an foremost, but I can turn me hand ta onythin in da case o an accident. Man, I'm seen me gaein fae slicin aff da blubber o a whale as big as a hoose, den jinin da lemmers ta sever da muckle heids, den ta da hert-men fur da diggin oot o da entrails an den, ithoot as much as a five meenit brak, mind, haalin da skeleetons ower fur da steam saas an da pressure cookers.'

When Dodie found out that his own fifteen-year-old niece, Gerda, had been impregnated by the whaler, he had to be physically restrained from going to the *black hoose* and confronting Gibbie. Gradually his rage settled a bit, but he was destroyed. Gerda had just that very year begun to come around the big stone house in which her two uncles lived, and had started to teach sign language to Dodie. To this lonely man, such interest and affection was like a blessing.

There was only one other person who affirmed Dodie – Andrina Abernethy, the woman who now lay at his feet. His roamings inevitably took him to her fireside, interludes deeply prized after bitter scenes with his alcoholic brother. Ten years ago at a Hall dance, Andrina did something which changed his life. Taking him by the hand, she led him to the four players raised up on a platform and, nodding to Jeemie Haraldson to keep playing his fiddle, placed her deaf friend's fingertips on the resin-dusted wood carving of its belly. Dodie recoiled as if it were a live thing. Laughing softly, Andrina urged him to try again. From fiddle to accordion, double bass and drums they moved. The dancers in the packed hall surged around the odd couple. Had Andrina taken leave of her senses? In between touching, Dodie rubbed at his hands and arms as though he had nettle rash. And then, to the gasping consternation of everyone, Andrina, stooping, pulled Dodie's shoes off and fisted down on his socked feet (two naked big toes scrunched in embarrassment). Lift and push, lift and push she went, and his smile widened as he felt the pulse and thrum and paradiddle of 'Da Hen's Mairch ower da Midden'. So full of imagery was the skirling screech of the tune that he could '*see*' hens scraping and pecking and stamping on a mound of kitchen scraps and byre muck.

For the rest of the evening Dodie nursed his great discovery. People observed that he was now and then keeping time to the music, his feet in their soft sand-shoes going tap-tap, tap-tap. And word went round that he could *feel* the rhythm of the tunes.

Some weeks later, at an island wedding – a grand affair for which a mainland band, wearing black suits and bow-ties, had been hired – a murmur of shock went round the place when Dodie and Andrina took the floor for a 'Pride of Erin' waltz. Tongues tutted as sentence was passed. Heads dropped like guillotine blades. Dummie and Bonxie glided and swayed and circled.

'She's geen cleen oot o her mind dancin wi yon fool bodee, makkin a serious spectacle o ersel.'

'Aye, aye, but whaur *little* is gi'en, *little* s'all be expected.'

'Aye, aye, hit's liklee da only man she'll ever git!'

'We shouldna laugh at dem, you ken; dae canna help it.' (this from two young men who did not want to be seen as mocking disadvantaged people). Dodie could not lip-read, but necessity had taught him to translate looks and gestures. He knew what people thought of him, and for himself he did not care. With Andrina's big soft hand in his, her sweet milky breath fanning his cheek, he danced, and was well content, grateful for this good woman's patience with his flat-footed steps. The love of a woman Dodie never expected to earn. Like Andrina, he seldom consulted a mirror, for he saw the reality, a fifty-five-year-old bald man with a lantern jaw and snuff-coloured eyes set in a face cross-hatched with lines formed by a constant struggle to make himself understood. 'A face only a midder could love,' his brother frequently told him in drunken bitterness. But Andrina smiled on him, and he basked in her kindness, holding on for dear life to her words, 'Doo's a *good* man, Dodie, an I *lik* dee.'

So, with a heart full of love and bewilderment, he crossed the road, shambling and peering and grunting. Fearfully, he bent over Andrina's coiled body and stretched out his good arm. The smells around her struck at his keen nose. Sniffing, he touched her shoulder, the gentlest of touches. She recoiled, one arm upflung over her face. He backed off, alarmed. He had words for her, but his tongue could not form them. 'Aheeah,' he said, a gurgling sound as though spoken through water, his face twitching and twisting. Hesitantly, she brought her arm down. He could see the glimmer of her pale round face. He smiled down at her, dropped to his knees beside her. His hands hovered over her like puffins trying for a cliff-top landing. The smell of whale oil and drink and something else he could not put a name to rose around him as she rocked to a sitting position. He felt the grasp of her large, soft hand in his and pulled with all his strength. And then she was in the circle of his arms and he could feel and taste the salt of tears, the heave of her muckle paps against his bony chest. Clumsily, he stroked her thick helmet of straight hair, bare of its beret, his phlegm-plugged throat croaking her name 'Aheeah, Aheeah' over and over, while the wind howled around them and the first fat feathers of snow eddied and whirled. Awkwardly he helped her to her feet, shyly swiping smoothness into her clothes. A shining thing at the edge of his vision. A heavy torch in a clump of heather. He retrieved it, pressed the stiff button and was rewarded by a long cone of yellow light. On a backward swing, the beam illuminated Andrina's solid legs, and his heart withered when he saw the ruin of her stockings, the spreading stains. Raising his strong arm, he made a fist and shook it at the road Gibbie had just gone down, and, squinting up through the swirling snow, growled at the sky. Andrina's face crumpled in a fresh bout of weeping. He found her beret, and motioning with the torch, indicated that he would walk her home. She did not refuse his offer and, with one last dash at her wet cheeks, she laid hold of her barrow, and swung it, teetering, back onto the road.

Their breath billowed around their heads as they pushed into the storm. At last the pair reached the cattle grid, and Dodie limped ahead and wrestled the gate chain free. Ruby had lit the lamps and the yellow light shone in the tiny, deep-set windows of their but-an-ben with its outhouse and peat-stack and hen-house crouched around it, whitening fast as though a giant fleece were being settled on them.

Never was the sight of home so welcome. True to form, the dogs in the outhouse had set up a furious barking, and as Dodie and Andrina began a careful approach over the rutted, unmetalled path, the porch door opened and they saw Ruby, hugging herself against the cold blast, outlined in a flood of golden light from a storm lantern swaying overhead. Dodie switched off the torch, hanging back awkwardly as Andrina trundled her heavy wheelbarrow and parked it by the dark boat shape of the peat stack. *Glindering*, he saw Ruby's face change from a welcoming smile to a wide-eyed stare as she took in her sister's dishevelled appearance. He saw Andrina's solid body seem to shrink and quiver and dissolve as she fell into the outstretched arms of her sister. Ruby appeared not to have noticed Dodie. But just as he was thinking that perhaps he should continue to the lighthouse for his weekly game of cards with the crew, Andrina turned to him and beckoned, and he entered the narrow porch and secured the door. He followed the two women into the warmth and glow of the but end and sat on the edge of their horse-hair stuffed resting chair, watching hungrily as Andrina told Ruby what had happened. Ruby's work-reddened hands clenched and unclenched as she stared into the tight face of her sister.

So many words for a thing which had been over in minutes?

The large brown teapot was on the Rayburn, its bulging cheeks gleaming, its spout with a twist of steam dreaming upwards. Gently, Ruby pushed Andrina into the sheepskin-lined depths of an Orkney chair, stood over her as she sipped and sipped, staring dully into space. The tea was good and strong and sweetened with condensed milk but the smell of whale oil was still in Dodie's nostrils and he could not savour the brew with his usual pleasure. Now Ruby was busying herself with the big black kettle, stoking the peats to liveliness, fetching a plastic basin from the porch, filling it, hanging a coarse white towel from the brass rail so that it swayed and floated in the updraught of heat. Realising the purpose, Dodie became fidgety and ill at ease, turning his body away from the stove so that only one bony buttock rested on the prickly bench. As the two women went out into the porch, their tortoiseshell cat crept from below the table and started to coil around his ankles. He reached down to stroke it and he could feel the thrum of its purring in his fingers and up his arm. Ruby came back into the room, butting the door firmly closed with her broad backside. She reached up to the mantel-piece, took down a note-pad and pencil, and motioned him to sit at the wax-clothed table. He knew what was required of him, and with tongue roving back and forth over food-masticked dentures, he bent over the paper. The pad passed between them, question and answer, question and answer, and after ten minutes of laborious scrawling on his part and swift, cursive writing on Ruby's, the tale was told and he saw the fury in her intensely black eyes, the pinched white nostrils and the heightened colour of her weather-beaten cheeks.

At last, Andrina, *happed* in a plaid dressing-gown, shuffled back into the room, and he could smell the sharp scent of carbolic soap. Again Ruby guided her stricken sister over to the Orkney chair, her own favoured seat, and rejoined Dodie at the table. Bending over the pad of paper she scribbled and pushed it across to him. With painful slowness, head rocking, he read, 'Bed for Andrina now. Not a word of this to *anyone*, mind! And thanks for helping her.'

But, of course, there are few if any secrets on an island, and gossip sweetens many a cup of tea. Ruby, who usually did the croft work so that Andrina could tend their shop, exchanged roles once her sister began to *show*. This unexpected turn of events was quickly and avidly noted, its meaning surmised, and speculation became *spikilation*.

Occasional glimpses of the fast-swelling body of Andrina were devoured, chewed over, spat out. Suggestions as to who could have impregnated this uncourted, uncomely woman spread the length and breadth of the island like an out-of-control hill-fire. Gibbie Tulloch, after three months of drink-sodden leave, returned to South Georgia, injured leg healed, liver severely damaged.

Andrina tholed her pregnancy with set features, and scarcely cracked a smile. Winter eased into a watery spring with young seedlings greening the land. A high-ceilinged summer saw the hoeing and heaping of early tatties and the singling of neeps, and in the circular *plantie crubs*, the lifting of kale and young carrots. Dry-stane dykers stooped and straightened, the chip-chip of their hammers vying with the song of the quarry-finch; and then it was hill-work with the raising and curing and barrowing of peats for winter fuel, while lush fields of silver-whiskered barley heaved and rolled and rippled for the comfort of sea-sick retired sailors.

But Andrina saw none of this. Indoors, wedged in her sister's Orkney chair, she knitted and knitted and better knitted, her large round head nodding to the rhythm of whirring wires until the camphor kist brimmed with snow-white drifts of shawls and *peerie* mitts and bootees and hats and matinee jackets and spencers – enough to clothe a screed o bairns.

On a hot day at the back end of August, after a fierce labour of five hours, the midwife delivered a nine-and-a-half-pound baby girl. She slid out with a grease-slicked flue-brush of sooty black hair and was soon fastened to her mother's milky breast. Dodie, who had sat outside in the yard during Andrina's labour, was the first visitor to hold the peerie bairn, his palsied head nodding and swaying in amazement, lips struggling to form words.

The bairn was bonny and blythe and placid. Daily, Andrina peered into the infant's face for signs of a likeness to her father, her loving instincts blighted by the dread that its plume of hair was not the only legacy. Dodie, a constant visitor, watched Andrina closely, the grooves of his face deepening with concern. The naming of the child was a vexation; Andrina felt that she had not the right to give her bairn a family Christian name. She worried at the problem like a dog at a bone, but could come up with nothing.

And then, one hot, hay-making day with lark-song drenching the air, Dodie presented Andrina with a bunch of lucky white heather and cyclamen pink heather-bells. Her brow cleared. She whooped. She dived across the room and clawed note-pad and pencil from the mantel. Dodie watched, puzzled, open-mouthed, as she scribbled and finally passed the talk-page to him, jabbing a fat finger at her words. Squinting, he read,

'Baby's name – HEATHER!' He threw back his head and cackled, sending the cat scrabbling for the porch. Andrina pulled Dodie to his feet, and whisked him round the tiny space in something between a jig and a reel, their frenzied dance fetching balls of fluff and cat-hair from below chairs, and causing dust motes to churn and collide in a sun-beam slanting low through a window.

Now, it was the time of the September equinox. On a *blashy* day of sea-spumed winds which raked and rummaged barley fields and put hens off their laying and cows off their milking, the sky over Gibbie Tulloch's bit of land lit up the hillside for miles. The tinder-dry thatch of his roof took fire. It burned and belched its black smoke, flames whipped horizontal by the gale. Two hours, and the dwelling was gutted, a four-wall shell, no door or window left intact. Dodie hurried to carry the news to Andrina. Ruby's big red face stretched in wonderment. Andrina's, in contrast, dusted with the flour she was using, looked like one of her thick round girdle scones. *How* could this have happened? There had been no year-end torching of the heather in these parts to send rogue sparks to the roof of Gibbie Tulloch's *black hoose*.

After savouring the full measure of this news, Ruby left the room to fetch in peats.

Andrina reached across the table. Dodie's face was still twitching and working with emotion. Stretching her fingers out, she stroked the puckered arch of his left eyebrow where the hair had been singed to a blond scribble. And she smiled, and Dodie smiled back, eyes glinting.

TIMOTHY PERTWEE
A Wish for Hussein

Hussein stood at the stern. He felt less likely to be seen there – everything went before him: the rest of the ship, his rescuers, the rescued, his father, and, somewhere in the distance, land. If he turned away from it, then all he could see again was the sea and the sky.

In one hand he held a bottle. He lifted it and made sure that the cap was securely tightened. It was morning now, so the stars had gone. Who decreed that a wish should not be told? And if told, who would decide then that it should not be granted? Hussein had not told his wish. He clasped the bottle against his chest and looked down at the furious white wash and then out along the foaming wake. He'd have to aim to miss the wash.

The first Hussein had heard of wishes and stars was out there. In the water.

'Hussein!'

His father had been calling him like this at intervals, in an increasingly weak voice, for hour after hour since they had been in the water, checking that Hussein was awake and had not slipped off the wreckage of the ship that had become their raft.

'Yes, father. I'm still here.'

'Hussein, you see that star?'

Of course he could. And he knew his father had been watching it too. It had appeared before the last of the daylight had faded. What else was there to see as the ocean below them and the sky above darkened? Even in the light, none of the other rafts carrying other survivors had been visible by the end of the day. They had either drifted away and were concealed in the swell, or had broken up and sunk like the ship. The pauses between calls from those other rafts had become increasingly long until no more were heard.

His father lay with his head cocked to one side. Hussein lay opposite him with one ear against the splintered wood. Neither moved as they spoke.

'Do you know what they say in some places about the first star you see at night?'

Too tired to speak, Hussein just tried to shake his head, though he wasn't sure it had actually moved at all.

'They say that you should make a wish, Hussein.'

'Is that what they say where we are going, father?'

This time his father was silent. They continued to face the star. His father must have learned this from one of the many foreigners he used to treat when foreigners still lived in their country. A time before Hussein was born. A time about which his parents sometimes spoke with the same wistful gaze they wore when swapping tales of departed grandparents.

Then suddenly they were leaving. When he asked his parents where to, they said only 'to a new life' as though that were the name of a place, and then glanced at each other, excluding him from their secret. All he knew about

'Anewlife' was that it was a long journey away. Hussein was also sure that the mysterious visitor to their house some time earlier was somehow involved. Hussein had spied from the hallway as his father handed over a thick bundle of cash to the man. His father's eyes followed the bundle on its path from his own hand to that of the stranger and then, as it was divided into two piles, into first one then the other, of the inside breast pockets of the stranger's jacket. The look on his father's face reminded Hussein of his sister's face when, having devoured all her sweets, she would watch Hussein slowly pick up the last of his – deliberately saved – and place it with the touch of a jeweller into his mouth. The stranger smiled, but not with his eyes, and extended a hand. His father extended his hand but did not return the smile. People almost always smiled when they parted with money: in the bazaars paying for food; at the ticket kiosk paying for the cinema; even his father's patients while paying for treatment, however uncomfortable. Not smiles of pleasure but rather of acknowledgement of a fair and reasonable trade. By the size of the bundle, Hussein thought, his father should be beaming.

Hussein saw the man on a second and final occasion, as they boarded the ship. Even though Hussein was with his parents, sister and numerous aunts, uncles and cousins, it was a relief to see a familiar face among the huge crowds squeezing towards the ship. A familiar face raised hope of order among the chaos. Once again the man was collecting money. Perhaps they would be at an advantage here as they had already paid him. But Hussein saw that his father again had money in his hand. They had to push and shove with the others. Those with the advantage were those that had now handed over the last of their money and were climbing the gangplank – a shambling huddle of hunched shoulders and overstuffed bags. The others, including his father, stretched out their hands like the beggars in the city, only here they were desperate to part with money which, anyway, would not serve them in 'Anewlife'.

'They say you should make a wish,' his father repeated, stirring Hussein from his thoughts. Or were they dreams? Hallucinations?

Why was his father talking this way? He did not believe in such superstitions. Perhaps this was the beginning of a kind of madness, the sort that afflicted those lost in the desert. Looking at the star it felt as though it were their own sun, abandoning them, so far away now that it gave no warmth. Its light was cold. The cold hurt so much that Hussein tried to remember the pain he had earlier felt in his arm which he had gashed as they threw themselves from the sinking ship. But, however much he tried, he could not bring back that pain. As the star grew brighter, the sky itself and the sea grew darker still.

> *God is the light of heaven and earth,*
> *His light may be compared to a niche*
> *in which there is a lamp; the lamp*
> *is in a glass; the glass is*
> *just as if it were a glittering star . . .*

'Make a wish, Hussein. But don't tell it to me.'

kindled from a blessed olive tree,
(which is) neither eastern nor western,
whose oil will almost glow though fire
has never touched it. Light upon light,
God guides whom He will to His light.

Was this what his parents had meant by 'a new life'? The promise of words written in the verses he remembered from the *Qur'an*? Paradise? Perhaps his mother and sister were there now. Did anyone know that he was here? He wanted to shout out at the darkness:

'I am Hussein, 10. I'm alone here with my father, trapped between the closing sea and sky. Is there anyone out there who can hear me? Does anyone know what has happened to us? Is anyone listening to me?'

Hussein thought that maybe he should hurry up and make the wish quickly. But which one to make? He remembered his mother hurrying them at the sweet stall on market day after prayers, telling them to choose something quickly. To make the wrong choice of sweet because he was being hurried would ruin his whole day, especially if his sister chose better. Thoughts of his sister hurt him more than the cold. There was no hope for her or their mother. His sister couldn't swim anyway – she was too young.

He was with them when it happened. Half asleep, his head rested on his mother's arm, soft and warm. There were shouts and someone pulled at his arm. Half asleep he ran or was dragged along a passageway and then out onto the deck. He never saw his mother or sister again. All that remained of them was a longing for the feel of his mother's skin and the relentless cries of his sister at home after he took from her a toy.

She had been playing on the floor in their room, alone with her toys. He knew by her different voices that something was not right. He looked in to see. In one hand she held her doll but in the other, confirming his suspicions, she held his toy soldier, to which she was giving the other voice as she introduced one to the other. Hussein ran into the room and snatched his soldier. His sister's dark eyes widened and now her scream still pierced his head; a scream which surpassed the countless screams of the passengers on the sinking ships.

One wish came back to him again and again.

'Hussein!'

Once again his father's voice startled him. Hussein was surprised also at the renewed vigour of his voice.

'Look, Hussein! Do you see it?'

It was dawn now but the bright yellow lights of a vessel sparkled like stars on the horizon. As the light grew brighter, the unmistakable shape of a bright red ship could be seen.

'Thank God, Hussein! Our wishes have come true!'

Hussein could only be glad that this had not been his wish. To have wasted his wish on something which had now happened anyway would have been too much. His wish was still valid. If only he could tell it to his father, not that his father would understand how such a thing. Hussein just felt a need to tell.

As the ship finally came alongside, Hussein saw that it was huge, bigger than the overcrowded ship which had sunk.

It looked safe enough, despite the red paint which Hussein could see was peeling in many places, exposing patches of rust. Their little raft rose high against the hull on the sea swell and then sank again so that the ship towered over their heads like a cave, up and down within touching distance of the fist-sized iron bolts.

The cap on the bottle was tight. The note would be safe.

Last night one of the ship's crew had given him a football. Hussein realised that this was now his only possession in the world. Not even the clothes he had changed into were his own. He had nothing else. He had had to leave many of his things behind at home when they left, and what he had been able to take was then lost with the other ship: his clothes, his books, his toys. His toy soldier would have sunk to the bottom of the sea with his sister and her doll.

He asked his father to ask the man if he could borrow a pen and paper. When they were produced Hussein covered the paper from his father's gaze and wrote down his wish. Writing it down felt like confiding it. It made it feel real. It gave voice to his wish. If he couldn't write it down it would be as though the wish had not been made. Who otherwise would know that he had made it?

'You are supposed to send a message in a bottle *before* being rescued, not after,' laughed his father as Hussein placed his letter inside the bottle. Hussein took no notice and went up on deck.

Out there beyond the wash was Hussein's entire history: his country, his home, his school and his friends. There was nothing to be seen of any of it. No sign either of the sunken ship. Nor of their raft. The waves were washing over his past life. The same waves which had sucked up the cries and screams until the only cry left was the one in his head of a little girl without a toy in a room back home.

Hussein raised his arm and threw the bottle as far as he could. It hit the water with an unheard splash and was lost in the waves.

MARK KILBURN

Greek Play in a Roman Garden

(i)

When Seneca was summoned by Agrippina to return from exile he gave instructions to his servant regarding his unpublished manuscripts. There were one hundred and seventeen scrolls in all – plays, essays, philosophical works, a biography of his father – housed in a cypress chest. 'Transport the chest to Lucilius Junior in Pompeii' Seneca ordered. 'I have arranged for your safe crossing. Here – take this money. You will be given more on your arrival.' The servant, a youth of nineteen, kissed his master and began to weep. For eight years he had cooked and washed and gathered fruit. In return he had learned more about literature and philosophy than was thought good for a healthy young man. Seneca's last words to his servant were: 'Remember – no one can lead a happy life without the pursuit of wisdom,' whereupon soldiers escorted him to a trireme and he sailed off into the distance.

Because he was expecting to die Seneca persevered with a work on cosmology throughout the sea crossing. With a favourable wind a trireme could be expected to reach the port of Ostia in a little under four hours. The journey along the bustling Tiber might take another three. The preferred method of execution these days was suicide which, if dragged out, would allow an hour or so for revision. Seneca reckoned he had enough time to finish his work on cosmology and dash off a final pamphlet into the bargain. He considered a subject for this final pamphlet. It would have to be something current . . . something pertinent to his situation. 'On Approaching Death' perhaps . . .

Arriving at the imperial palace he was ordered to wait in a room adjacent to the garden. He recalled that Agrippina kept him waiting when they were lovers too. She did this, she said, so as not to arouse the suspicions of her brother, Caligula. But Seneca knew otherwise. It was part of her armoury: Agrippina kept all of her lovers waiting.

She entered with her retinue of handmaidens and pronounced: 'You have aged dismally, Lucius Annaeus Seneca.' The philosopher admitted that Corsica hadn't agreed with him. Agrippina suggested they sit out in the garden 'where it is cooler and more pleasant'. Was there no end to this woman's appetite for maliciousness, he wondered?

'I have recalled you from exile because I have a job for you' she said. 'You are to be appointed tutor to my son, Lucius Domitius. You are to instruct him in rhetoric, public speaking and history. I have arranged for you to live here in the palace and carry the official title of praetor.'

Lucius Domitius, later to become the emperor Nero, was twelve years old. Already he had earned himself a reputation as a sexual exhibitionist and Seneca remembered the boy's father as a traitor, adulterer and perpetrator of incest.

'Have you anything to say?'

Seneca bowed his head. 'I am honoured,' he lied.

It seemed that the pamphlet 'On Approaching Death' would have to wait. But not, perhaps, for too long.

(iii)

The fishermen who had been hired to carry the servant to Pompeii were members of the same family. They took on board bread, meat and flagons of Greek wine. The youth was obliged to struggle with the chest alone. (Transporting a cargo of paper scrolls did little to fire this crew's enthusiasm.) A prolonged bout of drinking ensued before they cast off.

Seneca had drilled the moral creed of Stoicism into this youth. Throughout the years of the philosopher's exile they had slept on hard beds, taken cold showers, pursued regular daily exercise and existed on the simplest of diets. In the small stone dwelling where they lived they had studied long into the night. 'Cleanthes would never have been the image of Zeno if he'd merely heard him lecture,' Seneca said. 'He lived with him – studied his private life – watched him to see if he conducted himself in accordance with his own principle.' For eight years the youth had lived, studied and watched. And now, with his master gone, he was determined to follow his example.

As the boat journeyed the fishermen became more unruly. Thinking they were being tricked and that the chest contained jewels of great value, they snapped open the lid. Resigned to the Stoic dictum of accepting whatever fate may offer, the youth put up little resistance. On reaching the mainland he and the chest were unceremoniously dumped on the quayside while the fishermen went off to enjoy the pleasures of the nearest town.

(iv)

As things turned out, fate couldn't have dealt Seneca a better hand. His apartment was spacious, his salary inflated. The emperor Claudius, it was true, loathed the philosopher with an intensity bordering on the comic. But any fool could see which way the imperial wind was blowing. There were two contenders for the throne – Agrippina's boy and Britannicus, Claudius' feeble son. The smart money in Rome was on Britannicus fleeing while he still retained his head.

In the mornings Seneca tutored the odious Nero. The afternoons he left free in order to cultivate his growing influence. By moulding the youth Nero into an emperor who bowed to nature rather than the demons in his soul Seneca looked forward to a golden age. 'All men are born with reason,' he told his admirers. 'This is what sets us apart from the animal world.'

A message was sent to Lucilius enquiring after the cypress

chest. Yes, it has arrived, came the reply and Seneca made arrangements for it to be transported to the palace. He sent word to his faithful Corsican servant that a good position awaited him. But nothing was heard of the boy and, like other servants before, he was extinguished from the philosopher's mind.

One day Seneca discovered his pupil lying on the floor with a slab of lead on his chest. Nero explained that he had decided to dedicate his life to the arts of singing and acting. The lead would help strengthen his chest muscles. He was using enemas and emetics to keep down his weight. Apples – deleterious to the vocal chords – had been removed from his diet. 'I have gained permission from my mother to initiate a festival of the arts,' he said as he re-lacquered his hair. 'The festival will be called the Neronia and we will need theatre plays, Lucius – lots of them, written in the Greek style.'

Canace in Childbirth was to be one such play with Nero in the starring role of Canace. Seneca was ordered to start writing and dismissed.

(v)

After delivering the chest the young Corsican determined upon life as a simple traveller. He would roam the country in search of wisdom. He would visit great cities and spread the Stoic word. He would exchange the knowledge accumulated during his years with Seneca for bread and shelter. As he set off on his wanderings he doubted whether any man had chosen a more honourable existence.

In the towns and villages he met many different men of many different races. He learned of the pogroms against the Jews and restrictions on religious teaching. He saw great suffering and witnessed even greater injustice. At Capua he watched as a column of slaves was escorted to the gladiator school.

'The hand of Rome stretches far and wide,' a toothless Greek said to him as the slaves passed by, 'and its hand is an angry hand, curled tightly into a fist.'

The youth came to despise Rome. All men are born equal – Seneca had told him so. The Stoic masters had taught that mankind was a single community waiting to be joined in brotherhood. Yet hadn't the Romans created an empire based on inequality and exploitation? Even Seneca, its greatest thinker, had not been immune to Rome's barbarous nature.

As he continued his wanderings the youth determined to strike out against injustice: it would be a bold stroke in honour of future generations and in remembrance of his master.

(vi)

Canace in Childbirth wasn't the great success Nero had hoped for. His voice was too reedy and his wig kept falling off. The pigs' blood, standing ready in a bucket for the birth scene, was accidentally kicked over. After the performance Nero locked himself in his room and wasn't seen for three days. His tears, they said, caused the gods to hang their heads in shame.

He regained his composure on hearing of Claudius' death. Agrippina, tired of her lame husband, fed the emperor a mushroom laced with poison whereupon Claudius turned green, felloff his seat, and lay unconscious on the floor. His dinner guests, thinking the emperor was drunk, laughed and clapped at his witty antics.

Later, after announcing the emperor's death, Agrippina had Britannicus brought down from his room. She embraced him dearly, calling him the 'very model of his father' and advised the boy to remain in the palace. Then she sealed all the exits and sent wordthat the proscriptions could begin.

(vii)

Three years passed: Britannicus was murdered, Nero was crowned emperor. With Agrippina busy settling old scores, Burrus, a former army general, and Seneca became the admin-istrative masters of the empire.

'Tell me,' said Burrus, 'How do you reconcile the Stoic ethic of denial with your own immense wealth?'

The two men weresitting in the palace garden. A lazy ornamental fountain filled a lazy ornamental pool.

'It is a person's approach to wealth that is important,' Seneca replied. 'I have no need for it and treat it with contempt. I live simply and within my means. Tomorrow I could dispense with my entire fortune and still consider myself a rich man.'

'Then why don't you?' Burrus asked. He was curious about this strange philosophy in which wealthy men caused themselves undue suffering. As a former soldier, Burrus, a brave, hearty man, had endured much hardship in the field and was thankful now to have left it all behind.

'I hang on to it because it pleases the emperor. Am I to refuse him when he rewards me with great houses and estates?'

Nero had been rewarding Seneca a lot recently. *The Return of Canace* had proved a tremendous success.

Burrus again: 'But you're constantly contradicting yourself, Lucius – always having to compromise your moral values.'

Yes, Seneca wanted to say, I'm forced to compromise every time Nero hands me an estate in Lombardy or a grape farm in Gaul. I compromise when he has Britannicus murdered in his bed. I am constantly outweighing my duty to society with my duty to myself. And if I were truthful I would happily scurry off into retirement and leave Agrippina in charge.

Would history thank him for that? Seneca doubted it.

'I merely accept what fate has to offer,' he said finally, picking from a bowl of figs. It sounded weak and inconclusive but it was the best he could do.

(viii)

On reaching Rome the youth fell in with a group of cultists who worshipped Joshua, a native of Bethlehem. Joshua, they said, was put to death some years earlier, only to rise from the dead. He cured the sick and challenged the temple priests. The youth enjoyed this part of the story: Joshua striking out.

The cultists met in dark cellars. They held love-feasts and symbolically ate the body and drank the blood of Joshua whom they called the Messiah. Many of those attending were slaves, prostitutes and cripples: a brotherhood of man. The youth enjoyed hearing them confess their sins too. Sometimes he even confessed his own.

One night, soldiers arrived and arrested the members. 'What have we done wrong?' they asked. The sergeant explained that they were in violation of public drinking laws. The wine they were using to drink Joshua's blood was of the worst quality. 'It's for your own good,' the sergeant said. 'It's a hazard to public health this stuff. Look at the colour of it – it's worse than horse piss.'

In court the prosecuting council laid a trap and the cultists found themselves obliged to swear allegiance to Nero. The youth refused, claiming that Joshua was the one and only emperor in heaven and on earth. The others followed suit and all were sentenced to die in the arena. The youth walked from the court with his head high: he had struck out.

(ix)

Seneca pads across the piazza in the direction of the latrines. It's been a busy week – a week in which he has had to compromise his moral values many times. First there was a shortfall in criminals for the Neronian Games and Seneca was obliged to order a clampdown on religious sects in the city. He doesn't like doing this – let people find comfort where they can, is his motto – but he knows there will be trouble if there's a shortage of victims. And passive victims, found worshipping in subterranean caves, are better than no victims at all.

Secondly, Nero has finally disposed of his mother. The removal of Agrippina was politically prudent, and Seneca and Burrus helped the emperor concoct a viable plan. Nero lured her onto a boat which was designed to collapse. But the conspirators forgot that Agrippina was an accomplished swimmer and she survived. Nero, terrified now of his mother's vengeance, panicked and had her murdered by the worst kind of contract killers. It wasn't so much that Agrippina was dead that bothered Seneca – it was the pleasure Nero experienced after her killing that worried him.

In an attempt to lighten the young emperor's mood, Seneca suggested that he write *Canace in Love*. But the philosopher is having great difficulty in getting started.

(x)

The motley band of cultists is marched from the Mamertine prison to the Neronian Circus. As they make their way through the streets they are pelted with garbage and rotten fruit. The youth can smell pork roasting on a charcoal fire. He thinks back to his time in Corsica. His life had been happy there. He gives silent thanks for the time he spent with his former master. Now, though, he has discovered a new kind of wisdom and is prepared to die in its defence.

It is mid-morning when they reach the circus and the entertainment has already begun. A wild beast hunt is in progress. Nearby the youth sees gladiators limbering up for the late afternoon show. Then he is herded with the others into a secure area. A Gaul tells the cultists they will be disposed of around midday 'when some action will be needed to fill in the time.'

(xi)

Nero has ordered Seneca to attend, knowing full well that the philosopher cannot abide such bloody spectacles. There was a time when the emperor listened to his esteemed tutor and willingly took his advice. These days Nero has taken a liking to ordering Seneca around — as if he wants to remind the philosopher who's in charge.

How will I be remembered? Seneca wonders, doing his best to avert his gaze from the grisly sights taking place in the arena. It pains him to think of this. It pains him to think of Rome. Once he thought that he could guide men towards salvation. Now, he's not so sure. Each man must find his own way. There is no easy route.

It begins to rain. A canopy is hastily erected. The arena is soon heavy with mud. Seneca orders a servant to supply him with parchment and a quill. He will write an essay on friendship: something about the path to true happiness. In the rain, against a background of agonies, he dispenses with his cold Stoic creed and writes: 'If you wish to be loved, love.'

SUSAN SELLERS
Know thine Enemy

Miss Singleton stood on the top step of the porch and sniffed the air. A faint scent of molten chocolate assailed her nostrils and she turned back inside for her umbrella. It was a trick her father had taught her. If you can smell the chocolate from the factory, he used to say, you can be sure it's going to rain. Miss Singleton contemplated the untidy sprawl of children's bicycles and wellington boots that blocked her way to the umbrella stand. Really, she thought, squeezing herself past a muddy bicycle wheel, the place was going to the dogs! She would have to speak to the new tenants. As she reached for her umbrella her heel pressed on something soft. Sighing, she stooped forward to examine her shoe. A large white lump of chewing gum was stuck to the sole. She would talk to them directly she returned from her meeting, Miss Singleton resolved, prising the chewing gum free with the spike of her umbrella.

A plump woman dressed in a vivid pink sari showed her into the sitting-room. Miss Singleton sat on the edge of the sofa she had moved downstairs when her father died and tried not to look about her. That was something else her father had insisted upon. Never interfere with your tenants' decor, he said after she had complained about a poster in the hallway, lest they interfere with the skeleton of the house. He had bared his teeth as he said the word 'skeleton' and they had both laughed, though whether it was because of the absurdity of the analogy or the unexpected intimacy of the gesture Miss Singleton could not say. He had shown her how the poster was attached by lumps of what looked like plasticine that peeled away smoothly from the paintwork. Miss Singleton, remembering the chewing gum, pushed aside a rather grubby blue rabbit that a smiling, dark-haired child thrust into her lap and determined to be fair.

'Mrs Aziz', she began, wishing that the child would not keep reaching for the buttons on her skirt with fingers which she saw only too clearly were smeared with something brown and sticky.

'Mrs Aziz, I have come to talk to you about the mess in the hall.' The small hand caught hold of one of the buttons and Miss Singleton looked with dismay at the dark smudge that appeared on the navy and white dog-tooth check of her skirt.

'Mess?' Mrs Aziz seemed not to notice the damage her offspring had caused and was smiling benevolently at her daughter's small triumph. 'Mess?' she repeated, as if she were struggling to fathom what Miss Singleton could mean. 'Oh, the boots. Please to excuse. Always I tell the boys, put them in their pairs. But you know how it is with boys.' Her smile now was aimed at her visitor.

Miss Singleton stood up, glad that her sudden movement caused the girl to run to her mother in fright. The woman was impossible! She had lifted the child onto her lap and was stroking her hair. It was clear she had no intention of keeping her children in check or attending to the problem of the hall. Miss Singleton saw that she had no alternative but to return later and speak to Mr Aziz directly.

This war frightened her. Miss Singleton let the newspaper she had been reading fall back onto her lap. Her eyes rested on the solid frame of her oak dining-table. For a moment she saw herself as a child again, crouching under the table with her parents during an air-raid in the last war. She remembered Charles Wilson being hauled up in front of their class at school for drawing crude pictures of Hitler in his work-book. Yet the ruler had come down only once on the boy's outstretched knuckles instead of the customary five strokes, and she had thought then that it was because Mr Stevenson privately sympathised with Charles' drawings. After all, Hitler was their common enemy. That was the trouble with this terrorist war. No one seemed to know who the real enemy was. Miss Singleton sighed and let her gaze travel to the window. An orange blaze tore through the opacity of her net curtains and she got up in alarm. She walked over to the window and pulled back the nets. A riot of nasturtium flowers had erupted in the recent sunshine and spread themselves the entire length of the patio border. Miss Singleton frowned. She had been most emphatic with Mr Aziz about the garden. She had even insisted that the agents include a special clause about it in the contract. The grass was to be mown regularly and the beds kept free of weeds. She had warned Mr Aziz most particularly about the nasturtiums, knowing from past experience that if you did not root out the seedlings early they would end up taking over everything. Mr Aziz had assured her that she need not worry. My wife loves flowers, he told her, she will enjoy tending to your garden.

Miss Singleton went into the kitchen and switched on her kettle. She took the cup of tea back into the sitting-room, determined to finish her paper. It was another of the habits she had learned from her father. Do not be deaf and dumb to the world, he had told her, or it will be deaf and dumb to you. She took a sip of the pale assam and stared at the photograph of the young Osama bin Laden on the page in front of her. Fancy being one of all those children, she thought to herself. She knew one should never condemn another's religion, but really how was it possible for the children to benefit from a father's wisdom when there were so many wives and offspring to consider? She tried to plot the steps that had turned the awkward youth she saw posing in front of her into the evil fanatic now hiding in the deserts of Afghanistan. Of course, Miss Singleton reminded herself, not all the terrorists shared the same background. One had been discovered living quietly with his wife under a flight-path near Heathrow, just a stone's throw from her home.

An odd smell began to percolate from the flat below, the kitchen of which lay directly beneath her own sitting-room. Miss Singleton grimaced. Curry. Really it was too much! It wouldn't be quite so bad if they kept their meals to regular times. She herself always ate lunch at one and a light supper at seven. Now it was four o'clock in the afternoon. Once she had even been woken in the night by the smell. She had switched on her bedside lamp and stared at the clock, incredulous that someone should be eating at two in the morning. She had said nothing at the time but now she resolved to add it to her list of things to speak to Mr Aziz about when she saw him later that day. Feeling rather queasy, she pushed aside her half-drunk cup of tea.

That evening, after rinsing the plate on which she had eaten her two rounds of toast and lightly poached egg, Miss Singleton picked up her key and ventured onto the stairs. As she locked the door, she felt a sudden stab of pain at the back of her neck and raised her hand instinctively. Reassuring herself that it was nothing after all, she turned her attention back to the door. There it was again! A definite pin-prick just below her hair-line, only this time it was accompanied by the unmistakable sound of suppressed giggles. Her suspicions aroused, Miss Singleton leant over the banister and peered into the hall. Below her she could see two boys, trying to smother their sniggers. She recognised them immediately as the boys Mr Aziz had introduced her to the day he had come to collect the keys to the flat.

'What are you doing?' she called out, but her attempt at severity only sent them into fresh fits of laughter.

'What have you got hidden there, behind your back?' At this there was a great snort of derision from the bigger boy, followed by whoops of delighted glee from the smaller one. Then the door of the downstairs flat opened and Mr Aziz's head appeared in the gap.

'Boys!' he admonished, then saw Miss Singleton on the stairs above him. 'Good evening Madam,' he said, bowing slightly, 'I do hope my two naughty sons are not disturbing you.'

'Mr Aziz,' Miss Singleton began, but before she could

continue the smaller boy stepped forward and held out two gleaming, empty palms.

'See,' he said, looking up at Miss Singleton, 'nothing there'. Encouraged by his brother's bravura, the other boy now came forward and held out his own equally empty hands.

'Inside you two,' Mr Aziz said, and without further ado he ushered them into the flat and closed the door.

Miss Singleton stayed motionless for a few seconds, contemplating the space where the boys had been. Something white caught her eye. She went down a few more steps and peered at the object pushed back against the skirting-board. It was a blow-pipe! So she had been right all along, she mused, and went down the remainder of the stairs to retrieve the incriminating object. The boys must have dropped it behind them and then kicked it into the shadows hoping that neither she nor their father would see. Miss Singleton manoeuvred her way past the handlebars of a scooter draped in coats and was just stooping to seize the blow-pipe, when the door opened again. It was Mr Aziz, followed by the boys.

'Madam,' he said, 'I have heard it all, and now my boys are coming to apologise. It is most wicked.' He shook his head. 'Arjun! Gamini! Speak up.'

Before Miss Singleton could reply, the two boys chorused 'sorry'. Mr Aziz beamed at them as if they had just performed an act of exemplary sweetness. Then, one arm round each of their shoulders, he led them back inside. Miss Singleton, the blow-pipe in her hand, stood staring at the closed door in disbelief. The boys had wrong-footed her, damn them! She felt the rage boiling inside her, too angry even to remember the promise she had made to herself that she would contribute

20p to the church charity box whenever she caught herself swearing. Not only did Mr Aziz appear to think that the affront had been rectified, but he had made it difficult for her to embark on her own list of grievances. To knock now would make it seem as if she were incapable of accepting an apology. Heathens, she thought, laying the blow-pipe on the mat outside their door, and as she made her way back up the stairs the gawky boyhood face of Osama bin Laden came into her mind.

Next morning Miss Singleton set off for the market bright and early. She had sat up until late into the evening writing down all her complaints against her new tenants. At first she had thought of sending Mr Aziz a letter, but then the idea had come to her of leaving it for a day in order to distance the very serious points she needed to make from the events in the hallway, and then going to address him in person. It was Saturday, and the streets were quieter than they were on a weekday, as if everyone was still at home dawdling over their breakfast. Once inside the market square Miss Singleton went straight to the flower-stall.

'Good morning Bob,' she said, nodding to the man in the blue apron.

'Morning Miss Singleton,' the man replied, putting down a bucket of Michaelmas daisies, 'your turn for the flowers again? How about some of these birds-o'-paradise, they make a fetching display? I could let you have a dozen for a fiver.'

Miss Singleton looked at the bucket he held up for her and gasped. Great quiffs of orange shot with flashes of blue, the flowers were indeed like exotic birds. They were tall too, she reflected, just the right height for a centrepiece.

'No thank you,' she said quickly, and turned her attention to some white gladioli. Whatever could Bob be thinking of, she wondered, as she appraised the freshness of the blooms. On the whole he had advised her well over the years. Those – she fumbled for the name – bird of paradise flowers were hardly suitable for the church.

'I'll take a dozen of the gladioli and four bunches of the stocks, together with some greenery.' She watched Bob wrap her choice in a swathe of grey paper, approving the subtle mix.

'See you in a month,' Bob winked at her as he took her money. As Miss Singleton turned to go, her eyes caught the headline on the newstand. Anthrax confirmed, she read. Medical units on red alert. She clutched her flowers protectively to her chest and hurried past.

It was cool inside the church and Miss Singleton sat down to rest for a few moments before starting on the flowers. She had been coming here ever since she could remember. This had been her father's church and the building was as familiar to her as her home. She looked around her. Above the altar was the crucifix, and as she gazed at the body twisted in its agony she remembered the Lord's dying promise. She thought of the headlines on the newspaper stand and shivered. It seemed inconceivable that a simple package could unleash such terror. Delivered through the post too, she reflected, dropped into a box somewhere and then carried with the letters and parcels in the postman's canvas bag.

As she took the vases into the vestry to dispose of the remains of the previous week's flowers and to fill them with fresh water, Miss Singleton noticed a poster on the vicar's board. Goodness, how forgetful she was becoming. Tomorrow was the day of the host service for their sister church. It was a good job she had seen the notice and been reminded in time. Everyone would be there, the entire church committee, not to mention all the guests from St Anne's. Thank heavens she had not been tempted by those outlandish flowers.

Miss Singleton spent a long time over her displays. She always prided herself on her flowers, and tomorrow was an important day and she wanted to do herself justice. She decided to stand her vases on the two plinths on either side of the altar. She began by placing a tall gladiolus in the centre of each arrangement, and then adding four more gladioli at angles to the first so that the effect was rather like that of the spokes on a wheel. She trimmed the stems of the two remaining gladioli and set them in front of the central flower in each vase. Then she filled in the spaces, using the foliage to offset the delicate pink and lilac tones of the stocks. It took a long time, and when she finally stood back and nodded with approval at the effect, she saw to her consternation that it was almost two o'clock. She collected her belongings and hurried home for an unaccustomedly late lunch.

At four o'clock that afternoon, tired no doubt by her late night and the exertions of the morning, Miss Singleton sat dozing in her chair when a sudden blast of sound brought her to consciousness. She remained still for a moment, her head leaning against the wing of her chair, trying to disentangle the remnants of the dream she had been having from the increasingly unavoidable onslaught of loud music. She snapped her eyes open and tried to identify where the hubbub was coming from. At first she thought it must be the flat below, but then her ear guided her to the garden. Miss Singleton roused herself and went to the window to look. An appalling scene greeted her. Her garden, which she had so carefully inscribed in her tenants' lease as an item of responsibility, had been turned into a fair-ground. Brilliantly patterned rugs had been laid on the lawn and balloons of assorted colours tied to the trees. A table had been placed on the patio and was spread with a purple cloth, dishes of food, piles of paper plates and cups. There was a vase on the table into which had been thrust, pell-mell, long-stemmed daisies, purple zinnias, and red and yellow dahlias. Miss Singleton shuddered. She heard her father's voice. Dahlias are no better than weeds, he would intone, in response to their neighbour's show. Her eyes travelled to the rockery where she saw that loudspeakers had been set among the conifers.

A shout drew her attention. Below her, his upturned face wreathed in smiles, Mr Aziz stood waving at her.

'Miss Singleton! Today is a day of much rejoicing for my family. It is little Arjun's birthday. You see our celebrations.' His proud arm swept over the hideous assault on her garden. 'Please, you must come and join us.'

Miss Singleton turned away from the window. Come down indeed! They hadn't even asked her permission and there was Mr Aziz asking her to join in this outrage, for all the world as if he and not she were the proprietor! Fuming, Miss Singleton sat in her chair and seized hold of her newspaper. They were no better than terrorists! Taking over like this! They would have to go, she resolved, thinking with relief of the clause in the contract that gave her the right to withdraw from the agreement within the first four weeks if the tenants proved unsuitable. And the Aziz family were eminently unsuitable! She would ring the agents first thing on Monday morning.

Despite her decision, Miss Singleton found it hard to sleep that night. She got up early and dressed ready for church. Then she sat with the Sunday paper and read an article that explained the procedures she should adopt in the event of a chemical attack. Stay in, it advised, and seal any gaps in doors and windows with tape. Miss Singleton made a mental note to buy some tape when she next went shopping. Her oak table would be little comfort in such a calamity, she thought with a pang. She read the next paragraph and determined to add bottled water to her shopping list. Fortunately she had kept a large supply of her father's cotton handkerchiefs. They were of such good quality that Miss Singleton had been unable to put them out for Oxfam along with the rest of his clothes when he died. The article did not explain exactly how the handkerchiefs were to be soaked in . . . urine (Miss Singleton forced herself to use the word), but she supposed that when faced with such an offensive one might have to resort to drastic measures.

Her reading had made her hot. She wanted to open the window but the memory of the Aziz party the previous day made her reluctant to cross to that end of the room. Instead, she decided to go directly to church, even though it was absurdly early. She found herself longing for its cool interior and she still had the key from her flower-arranging duties.

As she walked along the street, the pastel harmonies of the flowers she had chosen began to lure her like a spell. She was eager to see them again, to drink in their sweetness and bury her face in their freshness. As she made her way down the gravel path that led to the vestry door, she spotted a white gladiolus lying on the grass. How strange, she thought, thinking of the white gladioli she had used in her own displays. She stopped at the door and rooted in her bag for the key. As she put it into the lock, she noticed that the door was already open. Had the vicar arrived, she wondered, in order to begin preparing for the service? But the vestry was deserted, and she realised with some alarm that she could not actually remember locking the door as she had left the previous day. She opened the inner door and peered into the main church. She hoped nothing had been touched as a result of her absent-mindedness.

Her eyes circled the building. To her relief everything seemed to be in its place. The green and gold cloth lay smooth across the altar, the embroidered prayer-cushions were hanging on their hooks, the hymn books were stacked in readiness by the front door. Only after she had ascertained that the main features of the church were undisturbed did she allow herself to look at her flowers. When she did so, Miss Singleton felt the blood drain out of her veins. The white vases were empty, looking faintly ridiculous on their tall plinths. At first she thought she must be dreaming. After all, who could have done such a thing? Then she remembered the unlocked door and the white gladiolus she had seen lying on the grass and a chill began to steal up her spine.

For several minutes, Miss Singleton sat very quietly on the front pew staring at the empty vases. She thought of the vicar, and the women on the committee, some of whom had already expressed doubts about her ability to continue to do the flowers single-handed. Others were forced to share turns, she knew, and it was only out of deference to her father's position as warden that she was allowed to retain the privilege of a turn to herself. And today, of all days, when there was a bigger service than usual to welcome the guests from their sister church, these fears were to be proved justified. She imagined the triumphant gleam in Mrs Sawford's eye as she stood to propose her retirement at the next meeting.

At last Miss Singleton rallied herself, and went back into the vestry where she opened and then locked the side door to the church behind her. Once outside her composure left her, and she began to walk, slowly at first and then more quickly, back down the street to her house. By the time she reached her gate her pace was the closest she had come to a run since her hockey-playing days as a pupil at St Matthew's School.

Miss Singleton shut the front door behind her with a feeling of relief. She stood with her back resting against it, failing to notice the shiny silver bicycle that had been Arjun's birthday present and which now added to the store of belongings in the hallway. When the tears came they did so abundantly, until her face streamed and the wetness trickled onto her handbag and then dripped in small puddles on the floor. Her crying brought Mrs Aziz to her front door, and before Miss Singleton could retreat to the privacy of her flat the wretched woman had wound an arm round her shoulder, and was cradling her head and stroking her hair exactly as if she were a child. Mrs Aziz led the sobbing Miss Singleton into her sitting-room and sat her down on the old sofa. Then, patting and squeezing her hand she forced the words out, until Miss Singleton had told her all about the flowers and the committee and the special service for St Anne's. When she had finished Mrs Aziz looked at her watch.

'What time did you say is this special service?'

The oddity of her question made Miss Singleton stop crying.

'Eleven o'clock. Why?'

To her amazement, Mrs Aziz laughed.

'It's only half past nine. We have over an hour to make two new arrangements!' She called her daughter, who had been hiding behind one of the armchairs, and whispered something in her ear. The daughter nodded and ran off.

Miss Singleton began to be annoyed. Of course they couldn't do new flowers just like that! Besides, it was Sunday, and the market was closed. But Mrs Aziz seemed undeterred by her protestations. Her daughter returned with the two boys who had used Miss Singleton as target practice. Mrs Aziz gave her orders.

'Good. Arjun, I want you to get the flowers we had yesterday for your birthday and bring them to me. Gamini, you are to take the scissors from the drawer and cut me some branches. Nice long ones. With plenty of leaves. Oh, and cut some of those pretty orange flowers that grow everywhere. We will use those too.'

At the mention of the nasturtiums, Miss Singleton forced herself to her feet. She was on the point of refusing Mrs Aziz's offer, when Mr Aziz, alerted by the children, came in to the sitting-room, carrying an armful of flowers. She saw straight away that they were the daisies, zinnias and dahlias she had spied on the table in the garden. He hurried over to her and took her arm.

'Dear Miss Singleton,' he began, 'there is no time to lose. The honour of your church, your name . . . We must go at once.' And before Miss Singleton could say anything at all, she was being swept along by his commandeering arm. His wife and children followed behind, bearing armfuls of her garden.

'Are these the vases?' Mr Aziz asked when they were inside the church, and when she nodded he began piling the flowers he was carrying into the empty containers. Mrs Aziz helped the eldest boy to arrange the branches he had cut, while the two younger children wound the trailing stems of the nasturtiums directly round the plinths. When they had finished Mr Aziz looked at his watch.

'Ten past ten,' he announced victoriously. 'See, no-one is here. They will never know. Now, dear Madam, you must rest. You have had a great shock.' Too weak to argue, Miss Singleton sat down on the nearest pew and bowed her head. At that moment the warden entered from the vestry and began making his way up the side aisle to the main door. He had a large bunch of keys in his hand. Any minute now, the congregation would begin filing into the church. With his finger on his lips, Mr Aziz escorted his family back towards the vestry, where his gestures indicated to Miss Singleton that they would slip unobserved out of the side door.

For once, Miss Singleton was unable to lose herself in the familiar rituals of the service. She managed to stand, sit and kneel at the appropriate places, but her mind had stuck on the garish horror of the flowers which, she recollected with a quiver, had been half thrown into the vacant vases. She dared not bring herself to look at them. Her name would almost certainly be struck off the flower rota. Worse, the vicar might consider the displays an affront, especially since, as Miss Singleton surmised from the loudness of the singing behind her, the church was unusually full.

Somehow she survived to the end of the service. She kept her eyes steadfastly on her feet as the church round her emptied, as if she were engaged in a moment of quiet prayer.

Finally, Miss Singleton judged it safe to exit. She stood up, still refusing to look at the flowers, and hurried down the side aisle to the door. To her dismay, the vicar was still there, talking to a group of people she did not recognise but whom she imagined must be visitors from St Anne's. Mrs Sawford was at his side, tittering at what she supposed must be one of the vicar's jokes. It was too late to turn back now. She tried to slip past unnoticed. To no avail.

'Aha, Miss Singleton,' the vicar called out, 'there you are at last!'

Miss Singleton felt how she imagined it might feel to be caught in a cloud of anthrax. Her knees trembled and she had a sick sensation in the pit of her stomach.

The vicar called again. 'Miss Singleton, your flowers!'

This was it. The virus had taken hold. She could feel it working its way into her joints.

'What a triumph!' The vicar beamed at her. 'So imaginative, so bold! Exactly the kind of cheering sight I've always said we need in the church. Young people are so bored by all our pale colours. No wonder they don't want to set foot in the place! Your displays set just the right note. We must show we are still vibrant and alive. That we have valid things to say for today's world.'

Miss Singleton stared in utter incomprehension at the vicar. He was gesturing now towards the flowers, which she realised were clearly visible through the open door. Her eyes followed his arm, and she saw a blaze of brilliance, an explosion of red and purple and orange that seemed to spill out from the vases and fill the space round them with exhilarating colour.

At that moment, a hot sticky hand thrust itself into her palm. She looked down to see the Aziz's small daughter. Then one of the boys came bursting towards her and she spotted Mrs Aziz waving at her from the grass.

'Mama says you are to come and have lunch with us. To celebrate.' The boy, Arjun wasn't it, pulled at Miss Singleton's free hand.

'Please,' he implored her. 'Mama says there'll be chocolate pudding if you come.'

Miss Singleton looked at the chocolate-hungry eyes of her captor.

'Yes,' she answered him.

LYNSEY WHITE

A Story for Girls

It's odd to be not wearing knickers, she thinks.

That morning she stood in front of the others and tugged them off, while Abby and Amy sat on the window ledge with their legs hanging open to show off their sprigs of curly hair. They had plumpish nipples, uneasy on loose new breasts. Soft hollow bras hung side by side on the back of a chair. They winked and giggled. One of them whispered: Look how bald she is.

Connie shoots up the stairs and slaps her nylon knees as they jump towards her. She last came this way an hour ago, one of ten excitable girls in new red leotards, tickling each other and twanging their black elastic belts. In the wings they stood silent and frightened. On stage, the spotlights startled the hair on their outstretched arms and they weren't aware of thinking at all, but only of moving, in time with the long, instinctual limbs of the girl in front. Then, safe and unseen as the curtain fell, the damp-backed girls went sprinting and giggling into the wings: they jostled together, sharing their sweat and saliva in sudden high spirits, and Connie felt fast hearts and hot tummies trembling against her. She'd never been so close to so many bodies before.

Now nine of those girls are watching an oily boy perform, from the wings, but Connie, the chosen one, has been sent to help Sigrid dress, and she shivers to think of it. All of the girls are in awe of Sigrid: straight-hipped, symmetrical, stronger than even the senior boys and at seventeen unreachably old. Spooned from one tongue to another her name is their ballet school mantra for talent beyond your wildest dreams. Connie whispers the word to the tops of the walls with their dark webs and, barely spoken, it sounds not like Sigrid but *secret*. It sounds, too, like the stories she heard about Vikings at primary school, when her whole class played at raping and pillaging all summer long on the sports field: girls with plaits and smocks, and boys in *papier mâché* hats with banana-shaped horns. They'd run home bruised when the sun came down, and drop asleep, dreaming of warrior men and their icy wives.

Connie bursts through the yellow-edged door at the end of the passage and into the sudden electric light. She rounds a corner and finds the white door, with its small yellow star, where Sigrid's initial and surname are inked on oblong card. She knocks and waits, with a dizzying breath in her chest. She stands so close to the door that her eyes lose focus and one yellow star becomes a constellation.

Centuries later Sigrid answers, impatiently, faintly. *Yes.*

The handle is sharp in Connie's palm. The door swings in, and the stars become one as she enters the room. The air inside is as brisk as winter wind on wet skin, and the light is the colour of knives. The blinds are up and the windows are open, even though it's four below freezing, and little pieces of snow are blowing in and temporarily turning yellow in front of the spotlights on the dresser mirror.

The room smells sour, like glue.

'Miss Nanette sent me to help you dress.'

On a stool with her back to the door, she sits in a white slip with a pale yellow hem that flits about in the wind. The cut of it shows a well-boned back and shoulders.

Tingling from top to toe at the sight of her, Connie's first instinct is to curtsey. Sigrid is breathtaking in the way that landscapes are, with her moon-coloured hair and her jagged dramatic pale face like a mountain or glacier. Undisturbed by Connie's arrival, she lowers her torso into the sickly hot light from the bare bulbs over the dresser. She dips her fingertips into a mix of powder and water, swirled together, and daubs her face with it, chasing the downward drips with the tip of a sponge.

Soft pellets of snow gust onto her bare skin and hair, but there isn't the hint of a goose-bump: she seems to thrive on the cold, as if she doesn't know that she's not supposed to.

Girls sprint by in the corridor, late for the stage. The thump of their pointes on the floor sounds uncomfortably close in the silence, suddenly broken.

'Who are you?'

Her voice is like skates on ice, like the softening scratches the blades leave behind them. Her vowels are sleigh bells.

Connie blurts her name, but Sigrid seems not to be listening. Instead, she lifts a wooden-backed brush from the dresser and beats at her breast-length hair till it crackles with static.

'How old are you?'

'Thirteen.'

Sigrid's eyes fix emptily on their own reflections.

All of a sudden she drops the brush, like a dog turd.

'Have you come on yet? I need a clean tampon.'

Coiling her silver hair at the crown, she stabs her head with a handful of shiny pins while Connie stares down at the brush on the dresser, its round rubber front and the loose spools of Sigrid's hair that are stuck to its prongs.

'I haven't got one,' she says in the end. 'I use sanitary pads.'

The words sound strange in her mouth, since she's never said them aloud before.

'You mean *nappies*?'

Sigrid jingles with laughter. Connie turns crimson. She's scared to use tampons: she doesn't know how, and she thinks that they stop you from being a virgin.

'How can you dance with a *nappy* on?'

Connie remembers the day when she couldn't, when Abby and Amy fell on the floor with laughing so hard at the sodden pad that poked from her leotard leg. Miss Nanette was outraged: 'You must be *dancers* before you are *women*!' she said. The class stood about with their arms on the barre and their bottoms relaxed, removing a pin from their hair or pushing their toe pointes into the ground, while Connie's hands cast about in moist nylon.

Sigrid laughs again, but quickly this time, like a whip crack.

When she stands, she's taller than Connie remembers, and very erect as if she's on strings.

'Is there blood on my legs?' she says.

Connie feels awkward, talking so openly. Most of her friends are still new to their menstrual cycles, and whisper in riddles.

'No, I don't think so.'

Sigrid snatches the white slip away and is suddenly naked, with buttocks like fists and a silver cow's lick of pubic hair in the mirror. She bends, double. Her spine stands up like a length of rope, her buttocks part and her tailbone points like the blunted end of a pencil, displaying her anus, snug in a silver coil of pubic hair, the way that peacocks show their tails or offer themselves for mating.

Connie squirms, and looks at the window instead, where the night is falling. She pictures herself in the same position as Sigrid: naked and shameless in front of a younger girl before dressing to dance a famous *pas de deux* on stage with a firm-thighed senior boy. She imagines the swirling air on her upturned bottom and backs of her thighs, and the warm sensation of being watched. Then she thinks about Tamsin, who followed her into the toilet once and told her to pull her whole leotard down instead of just squashing the crotch to one side. Connie wouldn't, and squirmed on the seat without weeing till Tamsin agreed that she'd face the cubicle door instead. There was blood that day on the lid of the sanitary bin and, worst of all, a man's thing drawn on the wall.

'Your turn,' Connie said after half a minute.

'Why don't you make any noise when you go?' Tamsin demanded, stripping and slumping herself on the hot plastic seat, with a vast red birthmark spread like a napkin over her belly. The water came out in a rush and seemed not to stop, while Tamsin sat patiently spraying, as brazen as dogs in the street.

'Shall I tell you a secret?'

Connie has never before heard a sentence so tempting. It

makes her forget that Sigrid is naked. She turns and nods, as fast as she can.

The wind comes in and flusters a few loose pins on the dresser: they fall to the floor, but Sigrid ignores them, touching her belly, pale and concave in the middle of parallel hips.

She gently inserts a fingertip into her navel.

'I'm not coming back next term,' she says, and time stops for a second.

'Why not?' Connie cries. It hurts to speak.

The windows shiver and snow floats in.

'I'm going to New York instead.'

'New York,' Connie whispers.

How can it be? It's the end, of everything. Six long heavenly months with Sigrid in reach have been shrunk to a single evening, and now they'll be light years apart for the rest of their lives. The moon leers in through the window: she might as well live *there* instead, Connie thinks, and her brain fills up with blood and her thoughts turn somersaults.

Sigrid fans her toes, like bird claws, on the cold linoleum: each one as long as the others, all swollen and rose-coloured.

Sitting in front of the dresser again, in the same pose that Connie first saw her, she spits at the glass and announces: 'I hate these fucking recitals! I don't want to dance with that prick Alexander. He had an *erection* at dress rehearsal this morning.'

She looks in the mirror for Connie's reaction, but Connie turns quickly to stare at the wall: she can't stand to think of men's privates, all purple and slug-like. The word to describe them is vile.

A flicker of interest shifts the features on Sigrid's face minutely.

'Don't you like boys?' she says, but Connie is silent.

Sigrid blackens her lips and blots them with paper.

'Well, guess what?' she says. 'I don't like them either.'

Turning herself on the stool to face Connie, she slides her legs to scissors on either side of its leather lap, and slowly the pale enclosure between them breaks open, exposing a scribble of pink and silver, lips and hair. It's like a large insect that seems to have features but no recognisable face. She aims her legs in Connie's direction.

'Watch,' she says, and a bright slug of blood comes away in her fingers. It meets the air with a slurp.

'It's a tampon, you *dope*,' she says to the look of alarm on Connie's face. She lowers her hand and the tampon slaps the floor. It skids a few inches and comes to a stop in the corner. It steams, like dung, and it stinks like Connie's backside when she hasn't washed it.

Now there is blood in the silver mesh of Sigrid's hair. She snatches tissues out of a box on the dresser and clenches her fingers together to make a white ball. She opens her fist, and they flower back to life.

'I've got an idea,' she says. 'Did you know that women in ancient times used to make their own tampons?'

'No,' Connie says. Her stomach feels hot, as if she's been standing too long by the fire.

'Let's try it.'

She holds out the tissue flower to Connie.

'I don't know how,' Connie whispers.

Sigrid makes a snorting noise. 'It's not exactly rocket science.'

But Connie shakes her head. The litter of pins in her hair grips onto the skin to stop itself slipping. Her brain is liquid.

Meanwhile, Sigrid is leaking blood on the stool.

'The longer you keep me waiting,' she says, 'the worse it will be.'

So Connie stumbles forward into the ice cold whiteness of Sigrid's body. Her longest finger is swathed with tissue paper and driven into the midst of the pink and silver lips and hair, where, like a Russian doll, she finds another, smaller pair of lips, but these are the colour of liver. Don't look, she tells herself. Her heart is restless and punches her chest.

But Sigrid says *deeper*, and swallows her finger whole.

The cold in the room is painful now, but the inside of Sigrid is hellfire.

'Why don't you open your eyes?'

So she does: it looks like a stab wound. Somehow she wads the paper together and stops up the leak. But soon there is less and less room for her finger: the flesh around her is closing in, and she couldn't be more surprised by the fat spongy feel of it. Connie has never, not ever, imagined that women and girls, with their long soft hair and their delicate hands and faces, might be carrying something like this in their laps: and least of all Sigrid. Pigs or cows, perhaps, would have centres like this, but not women.

She pulls out her finger: the nail is red, where the paper

tore. She'd like to wash it, but Sigrid is watching: her eyes are cold; unsmiling.

At length, she climbs off the stool and she looms over Connie. Her body is long and purposeful, like an arrow.

She turns Connie's nipples, as if to unlock her.

'I don't like kissing,' she says.

She finds the nook where Connie's opening is, and she stirs the red cloth with the soft underside of her finger. To Connie it feels like a pin-prick. In the silence she hears the quick march of her own breath, twice as fast as Sigrid's. Her body is heavy as chainmail. Her clothes are light as air, as if they might fly away or disintegrate. She is under a spell. Enchanted, she holds her tongue and is fixed to the spot by the might of Sigrid's middle finger.

As well as the tick of her heart, there's a new pulse now, in the place where her knickers should be, and she isn't herself anymore and every nerve in her body is drawn, as if magnetically, down to the friction of Sigrid's hand on the fabric.

'I can't do anything with you. You've got too many clothes on.'

Using her spare hand, Sigrid unpeels her, down to the navel, and wriggles her black elastic belt away like a bracelet. To Connie's alarm, her boyish contours shrug off the costume and make no resistance. Her nipples are showing. In spite of the cold her skin turns pink, from the inside-out, as if all the water inside her is boiling. Snowflakes touch her, now and then, and she melts them instantly.

The blinds bang suddenly left and right, and the windows rattle and free themselves from their catches.

Sigrid fires the black elastic belt at the wall, and thrusts her hands down the front of Connie's tights.

'How cute,' she says. 'You've got no hair.'

And, shocked into action, Connie's bladder bursts open, drowning her own sensation and Sigrid's hand in a warm yellow fountain of urine, as suddenly noisy as stones in a hailstorm, that soaks all four of their feet and the floor underneath them.

Sigrid springs wildly away from it. Swiping her hands on her legs and belly, she sniffs them disgustedly.

Connie begins to say sorry, but Sigrid is louder.

'Normally piss yourself, do you, when somebody touches you? God! I was joking, you know, when I said you wore nappies.'

She flexes her wet feet one at a time to show Connie.

'Look what you've done! You piece of shit,' she is saying, when, all of a sudden, behind the white door, comes a voice like the one that wakes you from dreams: 'Five minutes, Sigrid.'

And everything stops, and the clock on the wall with its scratched face shows them how late it is, and Sigrid says hotly: 'I'm not even dressed yet, for God's sake!'

It's hard for Connie to walk on her slippery feet. Her wet tights are saggy and making her sore, but she can't cry yet. On the back of a chair, in the corner, the dress that Sigrid will dance in this evening is choked in old plastic. She kneels to unwrap it, the skirt spinning stiffly beside her and glinting with millions of red and green sequins. Her chest is trembling. Her heart is out of step, and with every third beat it stops and waits for a reason to carry on working.

Sigrid is cooler, in every sense, than ever. She makes up her eyes: her hand is steady. She stands, stepping into her costume, revealing and sleeveless: its black bodice locks like a back-to-front corset and grips her slim breasts in wire cups.

She gestures to Connie, who hurries towards her and fastens the bent-edged hooks with her fumbling hands.

'You're a fucking idiot.'

Sigrid bangs her shoes on the stool. When she lays them flat on the floor, they swallow her feet exactly.

Arranging the straps of her bodice, she stalks to the door. Her face and her dress are meant to be seen in the dark from a distance: here, up close, in the room she looks monstrous.

'I want you *gone* by the time I get back,' she says, and then, like an afterthought: 'If you *ever* dare say a word about this, then the whole school will know that you pissed yourself on the floor, like a *baby*, in front of me. Got that? And clean your disgusting mess up, for God's sake, before you leave.'

The door sighs open. Slams.

Connie sticks her fists in her eyes. The room feels empty: the floor smells high with the stink of her liquid. She tries not to think, but from out of the blue come the people she saw on a beach, one day, who were being baptised: how they truly believed that the dirty water and seaweed coursing over their heads would cleanse them. She, too, wants to believe in impossible things. If she could, she would suck out the badness like venom, and then she'd go backwards: away from the door with its constellations, away from the passage; she'd tear down the stairs and she'd land in the wings, where her classmates are waiting, the slanted stagelights making the yellow down on their faces shimmer, like hatchlings. And Connie would bury herself in the warm damp mass of their backs, locking hot little fingers like bolts with somebody, while inches away Sigrid dances invisibly, hidden by nine excitable girls on their tiptoes, breathless and yearning, their fast hearts swelling.

Seconds later a curtain falls, and it isn't their hands or their faces, anymore, that she's thinking about, but their secretive soft-hard bodies, their marshmallow nipples and ribs like twigs, and their dented red bellies and flesh-coloured tights, and their missing knickers, all nine of them left behind on the dressing room floor, and she'd like to know who else is bleeding tonight and if they, too, have the same inferno inside them that Sigrid does; and, tingling down below in the place that she's got no word for, Connie feels somebody blowing a cold stream of breath on her body, and thinking of Sigrid she whispers her name to the tops of the walls.

But it's only the wind, after all, as it whips her pissed-on legs and the crotch of her new red leotard.

LES WOOD
In Memoriam

'I don't know who I am,' the man said to the boy.

'Are you a nutter, mister?' the boy asked. 'Only, ma Da says if a nutter talks tae me in the street, Ah've tae run like fuck!'

The boy stood on the road, bouncing a football, a Rangers strip that looked a few seasons out of date offering slim protection against the biting wind that rasped down the street. 'I don't know who I am,' the man repeated.

'You *are* a nutter aren't you?' shouted the boy. 'Luk at ye. Ye're an auld jakie. Where'd ye get they claes, in some minger's midden?'

The man looked down at his clothes – a rumpled shell-suit and a pair of holey trainers – they were caked in mud and what looked like fresh blood. He put his hand up to his head and felt slick wetness matting his hair. He winced as he touched a deep wound above his left temple. *Where did this come from?* he thought.

He wiped the blood onto his trousers and looked up the street. A grim succession of boarded-up tenements marched into the distance, separated here and there by gravel-filled spaces where other tenement blocks had once stood. A dog dumped a steaming brown mess on the pavement and trotted up the nearest close-mouth. Nothing here was remotely familiar to the man. 'Where is this place?' he asked the boy.

'Whit dae ye mean? It's Glesca!' The boy backed away. 'Ah'm gaun fur ma Da. He'll come doon an' boot yer melt in.' The boy kicked his ball up the street and ran off after it, vaulting a discarded bicycle lying in the road as he went.

'Wait!' the man called out after the boy. 'Wait! Come back! Tell me where this is!'

'You'd better run fur it ya bastard!' the boy shouted back. 'Ma Da's a mad skull. He'll fuckin' kill ye!'

The boy disappeared around the corner at the far end of the street. The man put his hand back to his head. He could feel blood trickling steadily. The wound hurt like crazy. *Was this it? This head injury? Had this caused him to forget things?* He tried to remember any recent event. What had he been doing yesterday? This morning? Five minutes ago? There was nothing there. It was as if he had been born seconds ago. There was no past before this time. The feeling scared him.

He looked around him. The tenements stood empty and derelict. Heavy wooden boards and corrugated aluminium blocked the windows and most of the doors. None of these surroundings triggered any reaction in him. Nothing that sparked a flame of the familiar.

Nothing.

He shivered. It was getting dark, and the wind whipped wet bootlaces against his face as it started to rain. He had to get out of here, find someone who could help, someone who could take him home – wherever that might be.

A few lights blinked on in some of the tenements. So

they were not deserted after all? Some poor buggers were living here? On the corner opposite where the boy had vanished he could see a red neon sign flickering above a doorway of a building standing on its own like a great grey shoebox rising from the surrounding wasteland. He turned up his collar against the wind and moved closer to read the sign. *The Herdsman.* The irony of such a name for a pub in a place like this almost made him laugh. As he got nearer, he could make out stark fluorescent lighting through the windows. No low-level intimacy here then. This was a drinking-man's pub.

Two youths stood at the door, smoking and spitting through their teeth as if some salivary disorder meant they had to empty their mouth of juices every ten seconds. Little specks of saliva joined with the first drops of the rain on the pavement in front of them. They watched him with smirking contempt as he walked up to the door.

'Where dae ye think you're gaun?' the one on the right said, blocking his path.

'I need to get in there. I need help!'

'Ah'll say ye need help. Luk at ye, ya auld tosser. Fuck off, ye're no' comin' in here lukin' like that.'

'Heh, Jimmox. Think he's got anythin' on him. Fags or that?' the one on the left sniggered.

'Naw, are ye kiddin' man? He husny even got an erse in his troosers!'

'Look guys, I've had an accident or something. I need to get to a phone. I need to . . . to get in touch with the police,' the man pleaded as he tried to push past.

'Wi' the polis!' said the one on the right, widening his eyes theatrically. 'Ah widnae go bringin' the polis roon here. Ur you aff yer fuckin' trolley? Goan, fuck off!' He aimed a kick at the man who stepped back just in time. The other youth moved in beside him and grabbed his jacket.

'You lukin' fur somethin' else pal? Eh? You wantin' a good kickin'? Cos me an' Jimmox here are jist the wans tae gie ye it!' He twisted his grip on the jacket and brought his face up close. The man could smell stale smoke and a sickening odour like rotting vegetables from the thug's breath. The man struggled, pushing back. 'Are you pushin' me? Are you startin'?' said the thug. 'You're fuckin' dead pal.'

'Look, please, I'm not starting anything. Just let me in to the pub. Maybe somebody there can give me a hand, take me to hospital or something. I just . . .' He was cut off by a head butt to his face. The blinding flash of pain was followed by darkness and the sound of merciless laughter.

'Boot his ba's!' came a voice to his right. He tried to turn and run, but hadn't thought yet to open his eyes to see which direction he was moving in. He staggered back and collided with someone behind him. He was gripped firmly by the shoulders.

'Lea' him alane!' It was a woman's voice. He opened his eyes, blinking back blood and tears. The two thugs were standing laughing in front of him. 'Ah know youse two. Jim Reilly an' Marko. Don't think Ah'm feart tae go tae the polis' cos Ah'm no'!' The woman turned him around, looked into his face with concern. 'Are ye awright, mister?'

She was in her early forties, but it could have been her twenties – he found it hard to tell in the failing light. Her hair was bleached blonde and she wore a cheap pink leather coat with a leopard-pattern fur collar. Her face had a hardness emphasised by too much makeup. 'Are ye awright?' she repeated.

'I . . . I think so,' he answered, feeling carefully to see if his nose was broken.

'Heh, Joan!' one of the thugs called out, 'Got yersel' a new man there? A right style guru that wan! Think ye can get him tae tell us where he gets his designer suits? Midgierakers Are Us?'

'Fuck off Marko!' she replied. 'A way hame tae yer weans and wife and act yer age!' She led the man away. 'Sorry about that mister. The language, Ah mean. Ah don't usually swear, but it's the only thing they type unnerstaun'. Scum, the lot o' them.' She directed the last comment over her shoulder. She turned back to him, looking with concern into his eyes. 'Did they hurt ye bad? Is yer face sair?'

'I don't know. I'm kind of confused. I mean I've been bleeding since . . . Well, I don't know how long. You see, I've . . .'

'Look, don't bother wi' that the noo. Come wi' me an' we'll get ye cleaned up a wee bit. Ma name's Joan by the way . . . well, ye awready know that, Ah suppose. They bastirts . . . Sorry again, but they bastirts jist don't know how tae be decent.' She took his arm and led him down the street towards one of the boarded-up tenements.

'Can you help me?' the man asked. 'I've no idea who or where I am. I think I've had some sort of accident, but I don't know what or when. I'm completely mixed up. I don't recognise this place or any of the people around here and . . . and I need to try and contact somebody.'

'Don't worry aboot that yet. Let's get ye sorted oot first. Ah've no' got a phone in ma place, but ye can get a wee rest there and get cleaned up a bit and then we'll see where we staun.'

She guided him towards the close-mouth and he hesitated as he saw the graffiti and broken glass in the entrance. 'Aye, Ah know,' she said. 'Hellish intit? Folk've got tae live in the likes o' this, an wee scunners like thae wans ye ran intae jist end up makin' it worse. Every night the same, brekkin' gless an' spray paintin' an' God knows whit aw else they get up tae. C'moan though, ye'll be awright.'

She led the way through the close and he had to step over dog dirt and a large puddle of what he hoped was water on the landing. The gloom of the low wattage light bulbs in the close made it difficult to see clearly. The doors to either side of him were covered in obscenities and gang names and he noticed that a couple of them were detached from their hinges. 'Do people really live here?' he asked. He realised how that must have sounded, and quickly added, 'I'm sorry for being rude, it's just that I . . .'

'Don't apologise,' she said. 'Ah wid say the same if Ah wis comin' here fur the first time.'

They climbed to the first floor and she fumbled with some keys at a battered door, green paint flaking and the window pane cracked and loose. She pushed the door open. 'Come in.' He followed her into what appeared to be an empty flat. An overwhelming smell of damp filled the hallway. Wallpaper had peeled and fallen away from walls stained with mottled black mould. Pale yellow light filtered through from the close landing. She closed the door behind them and locked it.

'Cannae be too careful wi' security roon here,' she laughed. She moved through to the living room area and lit a small candle on the mantelpiece. 'Electricity's cut aff.' she said.

He could see in the stuttering light that the room had a single mattress in the corner with a dirty floral duvet cover across it. The carpet squelched under his feet as he walked in. A framed photograph of a young boy of about eleven or twelve sat on the mantelpiece beside the candle. There was no other furniture. Some clothes lay scattered to one side and an empty cider bottle stood in the spot that had once been occupied by a fireplace.

'Is this your home?' he asked, astonished that anyone could be living in such squalor.

'No' really. Kinda temporary, if ye know whit Ah mean.'

'Who is that in the photograph?' he asked.

'Let's see if we can clean ye up a bit,' she said, looking him up and down. 'Wan thing's right whit they said. Ye are a bit o' a state.' She went into the corner beside the mattress and picked up a billy-can from the floor. She pulled down an old towel that was hanging over the living room door and poured the contents of the billy-can onto it. 'OK, let's start wi' yer heid and that cut.' She wiped the towel over his head and he immediately jumped back, his head stinging. The smell of petrol filled his nostrils. His eyes began watering, both from the fumes and from the pain.

'Wait a minute! What is this!' he yelled. 'That's petrol! What are you trying to do?' He pushed her away from him towards the corner of the room.

'Ya fuckin' arsehole!' she screamed, and ran at him, emptying the can over his head, and splashing fuel over herself.

The petrol soaked through his thin clothes to his skin, and he began to retch from the stench.

'What's going on? Why are you doing this?' he shouted through his choking gasps. He felt sudden, sickening fear well up into his chest. She came at him again, pushing him so hard that he stumbled and fell to the floor, slumped against the wall, legs spreadeagled in front of him.

'You!' she screamed again. 'You! You don't know who you are?! Well Ah fuckin' well dae! Ah know awright. Ye want tae know yer name? Ye want tae know where ye come fae? Ah'll tell ye, don't you worry. But afore that, ye're gonnae huv tae listen tae whit Ah've got tae say.' She circled him, kicking him back down when he tried to get up. 'First things first. Ye wurny supposed tae loas yer memory. Naw. Get banged up a bit, mibbe. Mibbe even knoaked oot. The memory thing's jist a wee complication that's aw.'

'What are you talking about. I haven't . . .'

'Shut yer fuckin' rip!' she spat at him. 'Don't let me hear wan mair peep fae you tae Ah'm feenished! Right?'

He nodded.

'Yer name. Yer name is John Steel. Ring any bells? Naw? Whit aboot the Steel Man? Big Steely? Naw? Naw, mibbe ye widnae get ca'd that tae yer face. Everybody's that fuckin' terrified o' ye. Though Ah don't how. Ye're no' much when ye're on yer ain ur ye?'

'I've got no idea what any of this is supposed to mean,' he started. 'Do you . . .' She silenced him with a sharp kick between his legs. He rolled away, moaning and clutching his testicles.

'Ye're jist no' listenin' ur ye? Ah'll say it wance mair. Shut.

Yer. Mooth.' She snarled each word through gritted teeth, the venom in her voice making the tendons in her neck stand out like pencils. 'Where wis Ah? Oh aye. John Steel. Not of no fixed abode as yer present appearance might suggest. Naw. The likes o' you don't live aboot here either. You're fae up the posh end o' toon. Bearsden. Big bungalow. Lovely cobbled driveway wi' wee lights up tae the hoose. Nice gairdens tae. Manicured grass an' things. No' like here. Nae smelly dugs' shites in your street. Nae vandalism or brek-ins. Nae drug addicts hingin' aboot your coarners. Aye, an' here we get right tae the nub o' things.' She knelt in front of him. 'Drug addicts. You never see the other side o' this dae ye? Aye, sure ye mibbe shake yer heid when ye see some pair soul oan the telly that's ruined their hale life wi' takin' smack or acid or whitever. Ye probably think, whit dae they start it fur? Cos they've got nothin' else tae dae? Cos they think it makes their life that wee bit mair tolerable? Naw, Ah'll tell ye why they dae it. Because they can. They can get it oan any street coarner or pub, or doon the bookies, or aff the van. There's aye a dealer somewhere affloadin' his gear. Ah, bit where dae the dealers get it fae? Where dae they stock up fae? Well it's fae the likes o' you, ya scum.'

The man started to sit up, opening his mouth to protest. She stood and kicked him in the face. He felt a sharp jolt as the cartilage in his nose cracked and splintered. Blood started pouring from his nostrils.

'Sit oan yer erse! Ye don't believe me dae ye?' she shouted. 'Let me spell it oot a bit clearer then. Fuck sake, this wid've been that much easier if they hudny hit ye so hard aboot the heid. Yer name is John Steel. Ye live in a big hoose in a nice area, drive three big flashy caurs, married tae an ex model wi' two wee lassies that ye send tae a fancy private school. Oh aye, an' ye import drugs fae South America. That's whit pays fur it aw. Everthin' ye ur, everythin' ye own, everythin' ye dae, it's aw payed fur wi' drugs. Don't get me wrang, ye widny dirty yer hauns wi dealin' or that. Naw, ye get some other scum tae dae that fur ye. You're the main supplier but. It aw comes back tae you.'

'No! That's not true!' he cried. 'I . . . I . . . I don't remember anything like that. Look at me for Christ's sake! Do I look like a drug baron to you?'

She laughed, a hoarse smoker's laugh. 'Naw, yer right enough. Ah cannae see ye sittin' doon wi' a Colombian gangster in that get up an' getting' any mair than a rifle butt shoved up yer arse!' She squatted down on the floor in front of him, put her face up close to his. 'The thing is, yer real claes ur probably getting' selt aff fur a tenner doon the Herdsman right noo. Ye see, ma two brothers, Malkie and Thomas, they're the wans that brought ye here. Bunnled ye up intae the back o' a van when ye came oot that fancy booteek that ye huv in the West End. A wee whack tae knoak ye oot, an' chucked oot in the street where they knew Ah wis waitin' fur ye. Wurny supposed tae send ye doolally though. By the luks ae that blood they skelped ye good.'

'But wait . . . wait . . .' He tried to stand up, but she pushed him back down. 'What's any of this got to do with you? I mean, supposing all this is true . . . and it's not, believe me it's not. Don't ask me how I know, I . . . I just feel it. But if it was true, why are you doing this? Why have you brought me here?'

She stood up and walked to the mantelpiece, the light from the candle throwing a staggering black giant onto the ceiling. 'Well, let's pit it this way. You seem tae huv forgoaten everything. Everything aboot aw yer drugs cairry oan. Well that's whit Ah want. Ah want tae forget it tae. Ah want tae forget the despair and humiliation o' huvin' tae beg oan the streets fur money tae get a hit. The needles. The disease. The livin' in conditions that ye widny keep a dug in.' She looked around her. 'Places like this.'

'But surely you can get help. Surely there are ways of getting off the habit that . . .'

She shook her head slowly. 'Ya stupid fucker. Ah've never done drugs in ma life. Ah don't even know whit they're aw ca'd!' She picked up the photograph from the mantelpiece. 'You see this wee boy? This is David. He's ma son. He wis ma son. This photie wis taken oan his tenth birthday. He wis deid five years later. That mattress yer sittin' oan. That stinkin' piece o' pish-soaked garbage. That's where ma son breathed his last. Shot up full o' your fuckin' heroin. You asked if anybody lived here? Naw they don't, but they bloody well die here!' Tears rolled down her cheeks as she gently replaced the picture on the mantelpiece. 'An' noo . . . noo Ah'm jist like you Ah suppose. You've forgoat everythin', an' Ah want tae dae the same. Forget it aw. Wipe the slate clean. Start at the beginnin' again. And this is the wey Ah can dae it.'

She picked up the candle from the mantelpiece and moved towards him. He suddenly realised what she was going to do. 'Wait . . . wait, you can't!' he shouted. 'Help! Help!' he bawled out at the top of his voice, panic constricting his throat so that it was never going to be loud enough for anyone to hear. He struggled to his feet, backing up against the wall. 'You've made a mistake! I'm not that man you described. I don't know how I know it, I . . . I just know!' She was silent now, advancing on him with a grim-faced certainty, the flame trembling and dancing above the melting wax of the candle. He tried to think. How could he get out of this? How could he get away? The door was locked. The windows were closed over with aluminium sheeting. He couldn't rush her – she was holding the candle. He backed into the corner. 'Please . . . please don't.' He heard himself sobbing. 'Please . . . leave me alone. Don't do it. I beg you . . . I beg you . . . I beg you.'

Her voice was cold and calm. 'This is it, Steel. Ah want you to die, ya bastard. Die in this shitehole lik ma boy did!' She rushed towards him. And then he found his answer.

He blew out the candle.

'Nooooo!' she screamed in frustration, as sparks of light flew up from the guttering wick: 'Nooo, you bastard, noooo!'

He looked on in fascination as a tiny fleck of light, a remnant spark from the candle, its glow fading as he watched, drifted slowly through the sudden blackness and settled where her outstretched arm must have been. There was a great rush of air as her fuel-soaked arm caught fire and suddenly the room was filled with a dazzling orange flare.

She stepped back in surprise, and he stood horrified as her other arm caught light. She made no sound, but whirled around the room, her arms held out stiffly to either side. He could feel the terrible heat filling the room and the stench of her burning flesh made him gag. She stopped beside the mantelpiece and turned to the framed picture. Still she made no sound, no cries of pain, no screams, despite the agony she must have felt.

The man made a run for the door, but she lunged in front of him and grabbed him as he passed, held him tight. He was aware only of a deafening bang as his clothes burst into flame. He struggled to get free, but he could not release the sickening grip with which she held him. He screamed, long and loud, but his lungs were filled with sizzling, crisping flames. His skin blackened and tightened, and still she would not let go, as he carried her around the room in a fiery dance. His pain spiralled upwards to levels beyond what he imagined was ever possible. Through the flames he could see her face, her flesh peeling away in bloodied layers.

But her eyes. Her eyes never left his. Even in this last moment she held his gaze and looked deep into him.

And then, out of the searing agony of the fire that encircled them, as his consciousness slipped away into a thankful oblivion, came the smallest of thoughts.

A memory of a memory.

He knew who he was.

AUTHOR BIOGRAPHIES

SUZANNE AHERN was born in Hampshire in 1964. She studied fashion design and marketing in London before working in consumer public relations for a number of years. Her first novel, *Joaquín's Dream*, was completed last year and she is currently working on her second. 'Sofía's Story' is her first prose publication.

DONALD CAMERON grew up in Coalburn and now lives in Law Village. A Master of Sciences graduate, he currently works as a Senior Biomedical Scientist. Half of a comedy scriptwriting duo recently commissioned by the BBC to write a pilot sit-com *Stable Condition*, 'Writing Wrongs' is his first solo project.

ANDY DRUMMOND is a native of Edinburgh and earns his living developing software for a Local Authority. In a well-concealed literary career, he has published articles on the Radicals of the German Reformation, translated books by German Socialists, and failed to keep his children entertained with stories of revolutionary turkeys and technophile hamsters.

ROBERT FREEMAN is a freelance design engineer living in the South Pennines. Born in Warwickshire in 1950, with one grandparent Canadian, one Hungarian and one German, it has taken the two world wars just to get here. He is a keen amateur writer and painter.

GRISELDA GORDON was born in 1961 and grew up in Edinburgh. Now in Ayrshire and mother of three, she is completing an MPhil in Creative Writing at Glasgow University. A classically-trained singer, she performs regularly with local operatic and dramatic societies. She is currently working on a short story collection.

MIKE GREENHOUGH was born in Derby and is a lecturer in the Physics & Astronomy Department of Cardiff University. In addition to research papers, he has had short stories published in anthologies, and has completed a comic novel.

ANN JOLLY was brought up in Glasgow and lives in England. She has been a probation officer, yoga teacher and counsellor. She has had short stories published in anthologies and is currently writer-in-residence at Dartmoor Prison.

ELIZABETH KAY has had stories published for both children and adults, and has had radio plays broadcast. She won the 1999 Cardiff International Poetry Competition; *The Spirit Collection* (poetry) was published by Manifold in 2000. Her first children's novel, *The Divide*, comes out in 2003, published by The Chicken House.

HANNAH McGILL lives in Glasgow and works as a journalist. Her stories have previously appeared in the *Edinburgh Review*, the Macallan/*Scotland on Sunday* Shorts Anthology and last year's Canongate Prize collection.

SYLVIA PEARSON is the love-child of a Shetland mother and a Norwegian father. Her short stories have appeared in various anthologies and she is currently nearing completion of her own collection in which she addresses contrasting themes inspired by living in Shetland and in South Africa.

TIMOTHY PERTWEE, a Spanish graduate, worked for a Spanish bank in the City but now writes full-time. He has recently been short-listed in a novel-writing competition and has been invited to complete his novel with a view to publication. He lives in Suffolk with his wife and two sons.

MARK KILBURN was born in 1959. After reading Drama at Manchester University he moved to Denmark and, between 1996 and 1998, was the writer-in-residence at The City Open Theatre in Arhus. His novel *Hawk Island* is published by Electron Press (electronpress.com)

SUSAN SELLERS is a Professor of English and Related Literature at the University of St Andrews. She wrote this story while on research leave funded by The Leverhulme Trust. She lives in the East Neuk of Fife with her composer husband and four-year-old son.

LYNSEY WHITE is a 29-year-old full-time mother. Having studied English at Manchester University she went on to live in London. Before motherhood, she had a variety of jobs in places such as a law firm, a virtual office and a furniture workshop. She currently resides in Norfolk.

LES WOOD is 43 and lives in Paisley with Marie, his better half, and Ghillie the dog. He lectures at Glasgow Caledonian University and is using what spare time he has to write a novel.